EXCELLER SELECT

TOP PICKS

YOU INC.

YOU INC.

VIEW YOURSELF AS A CORPORATION

DR. BHASKAR DAS

Book Coach and Editor

R. SRIDHAR

EXCELLER BOOKS®
A GLOBAL PRESS

YOU INC.

View Yourself As A Corporation

Cover by Exceller Books

ISBN: 978-93-47397-22-6

First published in India in 2026 by Exceller Books,
An imprint of GE Group
Address: G1, Dream Apartment, Degree College Road, Belgharia,
Kolkata, 700056, India
www.excellerbooks.com

EXCELLER BOOKS®
A GLOBAL PRESS

To My Parents

ACKNOWLEDGEMENTS

This book is truly unique—a wonderful piece of work, carefully shaped into book form by R. Sridhar. I was completely unaware of when and how these ideas and documents were discussed between Dr Bhaskar Das and R. Sridhar.

I would like to thank Sridhar and the publisher, Dr Sudipta Kumar Ghosh, for coming forward to publish this as a tribute to BD, as Bhaskar was fondly called.

Bhaskar was deeply influenced by his elder brother, Dr Ranjan Das, Professor at IIM Calcutta, who was his mentor. He also greatly valued the insights of Mr Samir Jain, Vice Chairman of The Times of India.

If he were here today, he would have wholeheartedly thanked his parents for bringing him up with such love and care.

He dearly loved his brothers and sisters—they were an integral part of his life.

He was a complete family man—loving and caring towards me and Rik, the apple of his eye, our beloved son. And Isha, the newest addition to our family, a lovely and caring daughter-in-law.

He was also deeply grateful to Mr Pradeep Guha, who was not only his boss but also a dear friend.

I thank the universe for creating a man like Dr Bhaskar Das. He is irreplaceable.

Thanks,
Somshukla Das
(Shoma, as I am fondly called)

FOREWORD

The Cheat Sheet to Life—From a Master Student

They say, Remember all the things you have been blessed with. Appreciate them. Be grateful. My friendship with Bhaskar Das is one of my blessings. If I were given just two words to describe him, it would be these: mind steroid. Conversations with him drifted from playful banter to fencing. The sword of his intellect and knowledge wove dizzying patterns. Every time it pierced through your defences, it didn't wound. It left you with a different perspective. A new wisdom.

He wasn't born with any of it. He was insatiably curious about what made what was and what is, work. Or didn't. Then relentless about how to make what is to come better. And he was as generous with all of it as he was with his single malt. Perhaps what made him a great teacher was that he made no effort to be one. He didn't subscribe to the notion that you were a mere jug, and he was a tap. The tap. For him, the transference of knowledge was give and take. He learned where you come from and gave what you needed to go farther. Faster. That was him. And he was most himself with young people.

This book is a great example of that. First off, it's not a self-help book. It's a cheat sheet that one great student passes to another, in the greatest exam we all take. Life. The only difference is that it doesn't have just answers. It asks questions. Challenges you to challenge your preconceived notions. Your textbook knowledge. And it does that by putting its arm around you.

The world is changing. Dramatically. At the speed of technology. How you navigate its swirling currents must change as well. Some say technology democratizes knowledge. Even some form of expertise. That's true. Bhasker argues that it homogenises it as well. In the soup of sameness Bhaskar gives you the recipe to turn yourself into a crouton. To stand out. Add the flavour of your skills that been honed on the sharpening wheel of new epiphanies, and your unique individuality to the mix.

I cannot recommend this book highly enough. In addition to reading it, I am fortunate enough to hear the audiobook editions of it from Bhaskar's own lips for as long as I have known him.

Bobby Pawar[1]

---

[1] Bobby Pawar is a story channeller, poet, advisor, former ad guy, and one of India's most awarded creatives.

Table of Contents

PROLOGUE

A World without a Map

Every generation believes it is living through unusually turbulent times. Yet there are moments in history when that belief is not simply an exaggeration but an accurate description of reality. I believe we are living through one such moment.

The systems that once gave life a sense of direction are changing faster than most of us can track. Technology is reshaping industries before institutions can respond. Artificial intelligence is altering the very nature of work. Entire sectors are emerging while others are quietly fading into irrelevance. The idea of a single, lifelong career within one organisation—once the unspoken promise of professional life—is gradually giving way to something far more fluid and unpredictable.

I grew up in Kolkata, then still known as Calcutta. My father's advice was consistent and unwavering throughout my childhood: study well, secure good grades, and find a permanent job. For his generation, that was not merely practical guidance. It was the definition of a dignified life.

I did not question it then.

But the world my father described no longer quite exists.

The Script Has Changed

For much of the twentieth century, professional life followed a reasonably legible script. Education led to employment. Employment evolved into a career. Organisations provided continuity, and individuals built their identities within those structures. Loyalty was rewarded. Patience was eventually repaid.

Today that script has been quietly rewritten.

The workplace is now a confluence of generations—Baby Boomers who built careers around institutional commitment, Generation X who navigated the shift from analog to digital, Millennials who rode the first wave of the internet, and Generation Z who have never known a world without it. Each group carries different assumptions about work, loyalty, ambition, and success. What one generation sees as dedication, another may see as stagnation.

And then there are the generations arriving next—Gen Alpha, born from 2013, and Gen Beta, from 2025 onwards—that will inherit a world that is even more technologically mediated, even less predictable, and even less patient with old ways of thinking.

The pace of change has accelerated to the point where even the most thoughtful observers are struggling to keep up. Reid Hoffman, the entrepreneur and investor, has suggested that the traditional nine-to-five job may largely disappear within the next decade as artificial intelligence (AI) and project-based work reshape how organisations function. Whether that precise prediction holds is almost beside the point. What matters is that it no longer sounds implausible.

We are entering a phase where discontinuity is becoming a natural condition—not a temporary disruption, but the new normal.

A Thought That Kept Returning

Over many years—through corporate life, academia, teaching, and countless conversations with professionals at every stage of their careers—one idea kept surfacing in my thinking.

It is deceptively simple. Everyone must begin to look at themselves as a corporation. A corporation does not survive because the world around it is predictable.

It survives because it adapts. It invests in capabilities, anticipates change, manages risk, and reinvents itself when circumstances demand it. It builds resilience rather than relying on permanence.

If the institutions around us can no longer guarantee stability, then perhaps individuals must cultivate a similar approach.

I have a phrase I return to often: *the past has no future.*

This is not meant to dismiss history or diminish experience. It is a reminder that the assumptions which shaped earlier models of work and success may not serve as a reliable guide to what lies ahead. We cannot navigate a changed landscape with an old map.

Leadership Must Change Too

This shift does not only affect individuals navigating their careers. It demands a great deal from those who lead them as well.

The command-and-control models that served organisations well in slower, more predictable times are increasingly inadequate in a world shaped by knowledge workers, digital collaboration, and the expectations of newer generations. Young professionals today are less impressed by authority and more responsive to credibility. They look for authenticity, purpose, and intellectual honesty in their leaders. They want to be led by people who are still curious, still learning, still willing to be wrong.

Leadership, in other words, is no longer about having all the answers. It is about asking better questions and creating the conditions in which others can find their own.

In many ways, leaders today must operate by the same principles as the individuals I write about in this book—constantly updating their thinking, refining their capabilities, and staying genuinely alert to change. The leader who stops evolving is as vulnerable as the professional who stops learning.

Why This Book Exists

The ideas in these pages did not begin as a book. They began as fragments—notes jotted after conversations, observations from classrooms and boardrooms, reflections after long flights, things I said to young professionals that seemed to stay with them longer than I expected.

Over time, those fragments revealed a pattern. And that pattern became this book.

I am not here to predict the future. In periods of rapid change, predictions age poorly. What I attempt instead is something more practical: to explore how individuals—regardless of generation, industry, or circumstance—can begin to think of themselves as self-directed enterprises. And how, by doing so, they might navigate uncertainty not with anxiety, but with a degree of clarity and confidence.

In stable times, people follow established paths. In times like ours, they must learn to design their own.

The chapters that follow explore how that journey might begin.

PART 1

The World Has Changed

CHAPTER 1

The New Generational Mindset

Every generation believes it is living through unusually turbulent times. Yet there are moments in history when that belief is not simply an exaggeration but an accurate description of reality. I believe we are living through one such moment.

I had been invited to speak at a management institute about leadership and long-term career building. The classroom was bright and restless in that uniquely youthful way—laptops open, phones lighting up every few minutes, conversations happening in half-whispers before settling into attentive silence. I had just finished explaining a framework that had guided much of my own professional journey: building credibility over time, growing within institutions, and steadily climbing toward leadership. A hand went up in the third row.

> *The student, introducing himself as Aarav, looked confident but respectful. "Sir, can I ask something honestly?"*
>
> *"Of course," I said.*
>
> *He hesitated for a moment before continuing. "Everything you said makes sense for your generation. But for us... I'm not sure it works the same way anymore."*
>
> *The class grew noticeably quieter.*

"Sir, my parents worked for the same companies for almost twenty years. But in the last few years I've seen layoffs, companies shutting down, industries disappearing. Even the most stable jobs don't look stable anymore."

He paused. "So why should my generation plan a life around one organisation?"

It was a simple question. Yet it carried an uncomfortable weight.

Another student joined the conversation. "Sir, for us it's more like building skills and moving where opportunities are."

I smiled. "That sounds suspiciously like consulting."

The class laughed. But Aarav shook his head. "No sir. It's not about consulting. It's about not putting all our identity into one job."

That sentence caught my attention.

"Then how do you define success?" I asked.

The responses came quickly. Freedom. Learning. Impact. No one said title. No one said corner office. No one said job security.

One student offered a perspective that captured the generational contrast perfectly. "Sir, Millennials believed in YOLO—You Only Live Once. They wanted to experience everything."

"And your generation?" I asked.

> *She replied with a grin. "LIMO—Living In the Moment."*
>
> *The room erupted in laughter. But beneath the humour was a profound shift in worldview.*

For my generation, work often became identity. Our organisations and designations defined how we introduced ourselves to the world. Yet these students seemed to be approaching work very differently. As the discussion continued, I realised their thinking was not careless or rebellious, as older generations sometimes assume. It was pragmatic and shaped by the world they had grown up in—a world of constant disruption.

Many of them had witnessed the COVID-19 pandemic during their formative years. They had seen entire industries pause overnight. They had watched professionals reinvent themselves in real time, sometimes multiple times. For them, change was not an occasional event. It was the default condition.

One student summarised it neatly: "Sir, our careers will probably change every five or ten years anyway. So we might as well design them that way." Twenty years ago, that idea might have sounded reckless. Today, it sounded realistic. History offers perspective, but it cannot be used as a reliable map when the terrain itself has changed. It is better to be pragmatic about it.

"A future tense is better than an imaginary future perfect."

The assumptions that shaped the careers of my generation may no longer guide the journeys of those sitting in that classroom. And that is not a failure of the younger generation. It is simply a reflection of a different world.

A Generation That Assumes Change

The workplace has always evolved with each generation. But Gen Z represents something qualitatively different from those that came before.

They grew up with smartphones before adolescence, social media before adulthood, and global connectivity as an everyday reality. They are what I call the thumb generation—digital natives for whom technology is not merely a tool that enhances work. It is the water they swim in. The environment within which everything, including careers, relationships, and identity, is experienced and expressed.

Watching that classroom discussion unfold, I realised something important. Gen Z is not simply adapting to change. They assume change. And that assumption reshapes everything—how they think about careers, leadership, identity, and success. Stability is no longer guaranteed. Adaptability is. Careers are beginning to resemble ecosystems rather than ladders.

I sometimes say that experience is a strange asset in such a world. It gives us confidence. But it can also create invisible blind spots. In rapidly changing environments, what worked yesterday may not work tomorrow.

> **"Experience can become baggage. The market does not value it as much as we imagine. What the market truly values is the ability to learn again—and again—and again."**

Work as One Part of Identity

Perhaps the most striking difference is how younger generations relate to work itself. For many in my generation, work was central to identity. Our professional roles shaped how we saw ourselves and how society recognised us.

But for Gen Z, identity appears more fluid. A young professional today might simultaneously be a marketing executive, a content creator, a freelance consultant, and an online educator. These roles coexist rather than compete. The idea of a single lifelong career feels restrictive in a world that evolves every few years. Instead, younger professionals increasingly see themselves as individuals managing their own evolving portfolios of work.

In that classroom, Aarav expressed it simply. "Sir, we don't think of ourselves as working for companies. We think of ourselves as building our lives." That sentence stayed with me long after the session ended.

A Conversation at Home

Later that evening, I mentioned the conversation to my wife, Shoma, over dinner. I was still turning it over in my mind—the ease with which those students had dismantled assumptions I had spent a career building on.

> *"These students think very differently about careers," I said. "They don't seem interested in stability the way we were."*
>
> *Shoma listened quietly before responding. "Maybe they're not wrong," she said.*
>
> *"What do you mean?"*
>
> *"Well," she continued, "look at the world they've grown up in. Pandemics, economic crises, constant technological change. Maybe they've simply accepted reality earlier than we did."*
>
> *I agreed. It was easy to assume that younger generations lacked patience or commitment. But perhaps they were simply responding rationally to a world that had become fundamentally unpredictable.*

Later that night, as I reflected on the classroom conversation, another thought occurred to me. Perhaps the real shift was not just in organisations or industries. Perhaps it was in how individuals now saw themselves. Younger professionals were no longer waiting for institutions to define their journeys. They were designing those journeys themselves—assembling skills, experiences, and opportunities into evolving personal portfolios.

In many ways they were already operating like dynamic entities that adapt, invest, and reinvent.

The younger generation seems to understand this instinctively. They are less interested in arriving. They are far more interested in evolving. And perhaps that is the most appropriate mindset for a world that refuses to stand still.

In other words, they were beginning to think of themselves not merely as employees... but as enterprises. That realisation would eventually lead me to a powerful idea—one that sits at the heart of this book. What if each of us began to see ourselves as YOU INC.?

KEY TAKEAWAYS

- Gen Z does not fear change—they have built their entire worldview around it. For them, impermanence is not a threat; it is simply the environment.
- Identity is no longer synonymous with job title. Younger professionals build fluid, portfolio-based lives and find meaning outside institutional definitions of success.
- Experience is valuable only when paired with the willingness to keep learning. Without that willingness, it quietly becomes a liability.

- The permanent beta state—a mindset of continuous evolution—is not a weakness. In the current world, it is the most resilient position available.

These ideas are not meant to be read and moved past. The generational shift described in this chapter is not merely an observation about the young—it is a prompt for anyone, at any stage of a career, to examine the assumptions they are still carrying. The questions below are worth sitting with honestly.

REFLECT ON THIS

1. When did you last genuinely update a core belief about how careers work? What prompted that update—and what belief are you still carrying that may need revisiting?

2. How much of your professional identity is tied to your current title or organisation? What would remain if both disappeared tomorrow?

3. What is the one capability you have been meaning to build for the past two years—but have not? What is actually standing in the way?

CHAPTER 2

The Algorithm of Disruption

There is a particular kind of unease that settles over a successful organisation when the ground beneath it begins to shift. Not panic—successful organisations rarely panic. It is something quieter and more unsettling than that. A slow recognition that the rules they mastered may no longer be the rules of the game.

I was meeting Vikram in his office after a leadership workshop I had conducted for his organisation. The company had long been considered a dominant player in its industry—profitable, respected, and admired by competitors and partners alike. For decades it had operated with the quiet confidence that comes from market leadership. Vikram had risen through its ranks steadily over twenty years. He was the kind of professional who did everything right—smart decisions at the right moments, relationships built carefully, a reputation that preceded him in every room he entered. By any conventional measure, he was a success.

> *Yet the anxiety in his voice was unmistakable.*
>
> *"Five years ago, we were the market leaders," he said, pausing as if weighing the implications of what he was about to say. "Today we're trying to figure out if our business model will even exist in the next five."*
>
> *"What changed?" I asked.*

He leaned back in his chair and exhaled slowly. "Technology," he said. "And the speed of it."

He pulled out his phone and opened an app. "This startup didn't exist three years ago," he explained. "Now they're doing what we do—but faster, cheaper, and entirely online."

I studied the screen for a moment. The interface was simple and intuitive, clearly designed for a generation that has grown up expecting seamless digital experiences.

"What worries you the most?" I asked.

He smiled, though there was little humour in it. "Not the startup," he replied. "It is the pace of disruption."

What Vikram was really describing was not just competition. It was the unsettling realisation that disruption itself had become continuous. And what made it particularly uncomfortable was that he had not seen it coming—not because he was careless, but because the signals had been quiet for a long time before they became impossible to ignore.

Over time I began to think of this pattern in a slightly different way. The disruptions appearing across industries did not feel random. They seemed to follow a sequence—almost like an algorithm quietly reshaping markets.

Industries are no longer reshaped once every generation. They are reshaped every few years often by companies that did not even exist when established players were drawing up their last strategic plans. The rhythm of change has accelerated beyond anything previous generations of leaders were trained to anticipate.

> **"Technology does not destroy industries directly. What it disrupts first are the assumptions on which those industries were built. Once those assumptions collapse, the rest of the structure inevitably begins to shift."**

When Change Becomes the Default

For much of the twentieth century, industries evolved at a relatively measured pace. Technological breakthroughs certainly occurred, but they were spaced far enough apart to allow organisations to adapt gradually. Once companies achieved scale and credibility, they could often maintain leadership positions for decades. Experience accumulated value over time. Institutional knowledge became a competitive advantage. Strategic planning could comfortably look five or even ten years into the future.

But the digital revolution has fundamentally altered that rhythm. Artificial intelligence, cloud computing, and advanced data analytics are transforming not only how organisations operate but also how entire industries are structured. Tasks that once required large teams can now be performed by algorithms. Services that once depended on extensive physical infrastructure can increasingly be delivered through software.

As a result, many of the barriers that once protected established organisations are steadily eroding. A small startup with the right technology can challenge companies that took decades to build. Competition itself has changed. In earlier eras, rivals usually emerged from within the same industry. Today disruption often comes from outside it entirely. Banks now compete with fintech startups. Media companies compete with digital platforms. Retailers compete with e-commerce ecosystems.

What makes this particularly challenging is the speed with which technological change now spreads. Innovations that once took years to diffuse across markets can now spread globally within months. Speed has become the defining characteristic of modern disruption. I sometimes describe this by saying that in the digital age, the half-life of certainty is shrinking dramatically. Assumptions that once remained valid for decades may now become outdated in just a few years. For leaders like Vikram, who built their careers in an era of relative stability, this shift is not merely strategic. It is deeply personal.

The Pattern Behind Disruption

As I reflected further on my conversation with Vikram, it became clear that disruption rarely arrives without warning. In fact, most disruptions follow a recognisable pattern.

The process often begins quietly. A new technology appears at the margins of the market. At first it seems experimental, even impractical. Established companies rarely feel threatened because the new solution does not yet match the performance or reliability of existing systems. Meanwhile, a small group of innovators begins experimenting. Freed from legacy systems and traditional assumptions, they test new possibilities and refine their ideas. During this stage, established players remain confident. Their business models appear strong. Customers remain loyal. Revenues continue to grow.

Gradually the new solution becomes faster, more efficient, and more affordable. Its user experience improves. Its reach expands. At first the shift is barely noticeable. Then customers begin to experiment. Adoption accelerates. And suddenly what once appeared marginal becomes mainstream. By the time disruption becomes visible to everyone, the transformation is already well underway. By then, the window for easy response has already begun to close.

I have watched this pattern unfold repeatedly. The media industry experienced it when digital platforms transformed distribution. Retail saw it when e-commerce altered consumer behaviour. Transportation witnessed it when ride-sharing platforms redefined urban mobility. In each case the disruption seemed sudden. Yet it had been building quietly for years. Which is why I often remind leaders that disruption rarely announces itself dramatically at the beginning. More often it begins subtly—and those who recognise the early signals gain precious time to respond.

A World That Is NAVI

One of the most significant consequences of technological disruption is the compression of time itself. In earlier decades, organisations had the luxury of observing emerging trends and adapting gradually. Today that luxury has largely disappeared.

The world we now inhabit can be understood through a framework I find increasingly useful. We are operating in what I call a NAVI world—defined by four characteristics that distinguish it sharply from the relatively stable environment many organisations once took for granted.

Change today is Nonlinear—events no longer unfold in predictable, incremental patterns. A development in one corner of the world can reshape an industry on the other side of it within months. Accelerated—technological advances compound rapidly; each wave of innovation becomes the platform for the next. Volatile—markets shift suddenly and without adequate notice. Interconnected—no industry exists in isolation; a breakthrough in artificial intelligence reshapes healthcare, finance, education, and retail simultaneously.

Evidence of this shift is visible in corporate leadership itself. According to a 2025 survey of over a thousand global chief executives, the overwhelming majority acknowledged the need to fundamentally rethink their approach to transformation—yet a significant proportion admitted they had not yet made those changes. In other words, leaders recognise the storm. But many organisations are still sailing with the same maps.

> **"Extrapolation is a lost art. The map of yesterday will not navigate the terrain of tomorrow."**

The Individual in a NAVI World

While industries are being reshaped by technology, individuals are experiencing precisely the same forces in their professional lives. Automation and artificial intelligence are steadily reducing the need for routine work—whether physical or cognitive. At the same time, entirely new professions are emerging. Data scientists, digital strategists, user experience designers, and AI specialists were rare roles only a decade ago. Today they are among the most sought-after professionals in any workforce.

This transformation is also giving rise to the gig economy, where professionals increasingly work across multiple projects, organisations, and roles simultaneously. A designer might collaborate with clients across several countries. A software developer might build products, consult for startups, and teach coding online. A marketing professional might manage corporate campaigns while simultaneously building a personal brand through podcasts or digital content.

In such a landscape, the ability to learn quickly becomes far more valuable than the ability to rely on existing expertise. Survival in the modern economy is determined not by the depth of what you already know but by the speed at which you can learn, adapt, and create value in new contexts. Those who cultivate curiosity and genuine openness to new ideas develop a powerful advantage. Those who assume that past knowledge will remain sufficient often find themselves struggling to keep pace.

Anticipating the Future

A few days after that meeting with Vikram, I mentioned the conversation to my son Rik during a phone call. He had always had a sharper read on technology than I did, and I was curious what he made of the anxiety I had witnessed.

> *"They're worried about startups disrupting them," I told him.*
>
> *Rik laughed gently. "That's not the real disruption, Dad."*
>
> *"What do you mean?"*
>
> *"The real disruption," he explained, "is that technology keeps lowering the barriers for the next startup. Every wave makes the next one easier."*
>
> *I thought about that for a moment. "So it never stabilises?"*
>
> *"Not in the way they're hoping for," he said. "Each technological advance becomes a platform for the next one. Cloud computing, AI, digital distribution—they compound. The disruption doesn't end. It accelerates."*
>
> *There was a pause before he added: "The companies that survive won't be the ones that defended their position. They'll be the ones that kept building."*

His observation captured the essence of the challenge. Each technological advance becomes a platform for further innovation. Together they create an environment in which innovation compounds rapidly. In such a world, disruption is not an isolated event. It is the environment itself.

Once we begin to recognise this pattern, disruption starts to resemble something almost systematic—like an algorithm. New technologies emerge. Innovators experiment. Customers adopt new behaviours. Markets reorganise. Understanding this pattern does not eliminate uncertainty. But it does provide perspective.

Because when we recognise patterns, we can prepare for them rather than simply react to them.

For individuals, it raises an important question. If disruption behaves like an algorithm, how should we design ourselves to thrive within it? That question leads us to the central idea of this book. Because in a world where industries transform rapidly and certainty fades quickly, the most resilient strategy may be to think of ourselves not merely as employees—but as evolving enterprises. As YOU INC.

KEY TAKEAWAYS

- Disruption follows a pattern—quiet emergence, gradual acceleration, sudden mainstream arrival. Those who learn to recognise the early signals gain precious time to respond.
- Technology does not destroy industries outright. It first dismantles the assumptions on which those industries were built. When the assumptions collapse, the structure follows.
- We live in a NAVI world—Nonlinear, Accelerated, Volatile, Interconnected. Stability can no longer be assumed; adaptability must be actively cultivated.
- For individuals, the implication is direct: learning speed matters more than accumulated expertise. The ability to evolve continuously is the defining professional skill of our time.

Disruption, as we have seen, is not a single event. It is the environment. The chapters ahead explore how individuals can design themselves to navigate that environment—not by predicting what comes next, but by building the capacity to respond to whatever does.

REFLECT ON THIS

1. Is there an assumption at the heart of your current career or industry that has quietly stopped being reliable? What would it mean to let go of it?
2. When disruption arrived in your field, were you among those who saw it early—or among those who recognised it only once it was impossible to ignore? What made the difference?
3. What is one thing you are currently doing primarily because it has always worked—and not because you have recently tested whether it still does?

CHAPTER 3

Living in a World without Permanence

Of all the shifts described in this book, the one that catches people most off guard is not the speed of technological change, or the restlessness of the younger generation. It is the quiet disappearance of something that most professionals never thought to question: the assumption of continuity.

For most of the twentieth century, a career was built on the understanding that if you performed well and remained loyal, the institution would hold. That understanding shaped not just professional choices but entire lives—homes purchased, children educated, retirements planned. The phone call I received one morning reminded me, in a very personal way, of how completely that understanding has unravelled.

> *The voice on the phone sounded unusually subdued. It was a former colleague of mine—an accomplished professional who had spent more than two decades building his career within a single organisation. Over the years he had risen steadily through the ranks, earned the respect of his peers, and developed deep expertise in his field. In many ways he represented what success had traditionally looked like: dedication, consistency, and long-term commitment to one institution.*

> *"What happened?" I asked.*
>
> *"Our division is being restructured," he replied. "They say the business is moving in a different direction."*
>
> *There was a brief silence before he added quietly, "My role no longer exists."*
>
> *The words carried a sense of disbelief. For years his career had followed a familiar and predictable trajectory. Promotions had arrived at expected intervals, responsibilities had expanded gradually, and the organisation he served had appeared solid—almost permanent.*
>
> *Yet within a few months everything had changed.*
>
> *"I never thought it would happen to me," he said.*

After we ended the call, I found myself reflecting on how familiar this story had become. Across industries and professions, similar conversations were unfolding. Organisations were restructuring, merging, automating, and reinventing themselves at a pace few had anticipated. Entire divisions were being reimagined. Roles that had once seemed essential were quietly disappearing. What once felt stable was now fluid. And permanence—once the invisible foundation of professional life—was slowly fading away.

The Disappearing Promise of Stability

For much of the twentieth century careers appeared stable because change moved slowly. Organisations evolved over decades rather than years, and roles remained relevant long enough for individuals to build entire professional lives around them. People joined companies early in their careers and progressed gradually through the hierarchy. Loyalty was rewarded with security, and security created the confidence required for long-term planning.

Families made life decisions around this assumption of stability. Homes were purchased on the basis of predictable income growth. Children's education was planned with the expectation that careers would unfold steadily over time. Retirement plans were built on the belief that institutions themselves would endure.

But the forces reshaping our world have steadily eroded that model. In the NAVI world we discussed earlier—where change is nonlinear, accelerated, volatile and interconnected—industries transform faster than traditional career structures can keep pace with. Technologies evolve continuously. Markets shift rapidly. Consumer behaviour changes with remarkable speed. Under such conditions organisations must reinvent themselves repeatedly in order to survive. And when organisations reinvent themselves, the roles within them inevitably evolve as well. Some roles expand. Some transform into entirely new responsibilities. And some quietly disappear.

This reality does not necessarily reflect failure on the part of the individual. More often it reflects the nature of an environment where change has become continuous. Organisations do not eliminate talent as frequently as they eliminate roles. Roles are designed around particular circumstances. When those circumstances change, the roles inevitably change with them. Understanding this distinction can make disruption easier to navigate. Because it shifts the focus away from protecting a specific position and toward strengthening the underlying capabilities that make an individual valuable in any context.

> **"The individual's kingdom lies where discontinuity and death are embraced with equal ease. This is not a counsel of resignation; it is a description of a particular kind of inner freedom.**

The Shrinking Half-Life of Skills

Another reality shaping modern careers is the rapid shortening of what some thinkers call the half-life of skills. In earlier decades, knowledge remained relevant for long periods. A qualification acquired at the beginning of a career could sustain an individual for many years with only incremental updates. Today, that cycle has accelerated dramatically.

In several industries, the half-life of professional skills is estimated at five years or less. This means that within a relatively short time, a significant portion of what we know may become outdated or insufficient. Technologies evolve. Business models shift. Entire industries are reconfigured. Under such conditions the challenge facing professionals is not merely acquiring expertise once. It is renewing that expertise continuously. Learning can no longer be an occasional activity undertaken at the beginning of a career. It must become an ongoing discipline. In the NAVI world, relevance is not preserved automatically. It must be actively maintained.

From Dependence to Self-Direction

These changes require a fundamental shift in mindset. In the past, many professionals relied heavily on organisations to define their growth path. Career progression was structured through formal hierarchies, and the institution itself provided direction, training, and opportunities for advancement. Today, that responsibility increasingly rests with the individual.

Professionals must think beyond the boundaries of their current job descriptions and consider the broader trajectory of their capabilities. They must ask themselves questions that earlier generations rarely needed to confront so explicitly. *What skills am I building today that will remain valuable tomorrow? How adaptable are those skills across industries? What new capabilities will I need five years from now?* In other words, careers can no longer be managed passively. They must be designed intentionally.

Increasingly, professionals are discovering that their careers may not unfold within a single institutional structure. Instead, they may move across organisations, industries, and even professions over the course of their working lives. Some combine multiple roles simultaneously—advisory assignments, entrepreneurial ventures, consulting engagements, and creative pursuits. In many ways, careers are beginning to resemble investment portfolios rather than single long-term deposits.

Lessons from a Footpath Enterprise

A few days after my conversation with my colleague, I was waiting outside an office building for my driver to arrive. It was early evening, that busy hour when the city seems to move in several directions at once. Office workers were stepping out of glass towers, traffic had begun its familiar chorus of horns, and roadside vendors were preparing for the evening rush. A little distance away, a teenage boy was running a small chai stall on the footpath.

> *At first glance there was nothing remarkable about it. A steel kettle rested on a small gas burner. Several glasses were arranged neatly on a tray. A jar of biscuits stood beside a small container of sugar and tea leaves.*

Yet as I stood there watching him, I began to notice something interesting. He was managing everything himself. He greeted customers with easy familiarity, remembered who preferred less sugar, who liked their tea stronger, and who was in a hurry. While the tea simmered, he counted change quickly and accurately. Every few minutes he stepped aside briefly to refill water from a nearby tap.

When a regular customer arrived, he smiled and said, "Two minutes, bhaiya. Fresh bana raha hoon."

The customer nodded patiently.

The boy was perhaps 16 or 17, yet in those few minutes he was simultaneously managing production, customer relationships, inventory, pricing, and cash flow.

When my tea arrived, I asked him how long he had been doing this.

"Two years," he replied.

"And you manage it alone?"

He nodded. "Morning mein school tha," he added. "Abhi evening mein chai bechta hoon."

> *His answer was simple, almost casual. But what struck me was not merely his industriousness. It was his clarity. Without using the language of management theory, he understood something essential: value is created when you solve problems for people.*

The office workers who stopped by his stall were not merely buying tea. They were buying convenience, familiarity, and a moment of pause in a busy evening. The boy had organised his small enterprise around delivering that value efficiently. In essence, he had grasped something that many professionals overlook. The ability to create value does not come from a designation. It comes from understanding needs and responding to them effectively.

As the evening crowd gathered around his small stall, I realised that the ability to organise one's skills, resources, and relationships independently may become one of the most important capabilities in the uncertain world ahead. In many ways that young boy on the footpath had already begun doing something that modern professionals are only starting to understand. He was managing his own enterprise.

> **"The temptation is to manage the future from the present, rather than manage the present from the future. The wiser practice is to start from a clear sense of who you want to become."**

The Individual as the Constant

If institutions are no longer permanent, then what remains constant? The answer lies with the individual. Organisations may transform, industries may evolve, and technologies may advance, but individuals carry their knowledge, relationships, and capabilities with them throughout their professional journeys. This makes personal development more important than ever before.

In many ways, professionals must begin to think of themselves as dynamic enterprises—continuously evolving systems that manage their own growth and adaptation. Successful organisations invest in research and development because they understand that innovation ensures long-term survival. In much the same way individuals must invest continuously in learning and skill development. Organisations cultivate networks of partners and collaborators to expand their opportunities. Individuals must do the same by building meaningful professional relationships. Institutions may offer employment, but only individuals can build enduring relevance.

Later that week I mentioned my colleague's situation during dinner at home. "It's unsettling," I told Shoma. "Someone can do everything right for twenty years and still find their role disappearing." She listened quietly before responding. "Maybe the mistake," she said, "is expecting permanence in the first place." True, I told myself. For generations stability had been treated almost as an entitlement. But perhaps the world had changed in ways that made such expectations unrealistic. Instead of seeking permanence, perhaps the real challenge was learning to navigate uncertainty with confidence.

KEY TAKEAWAYS

- Permanence was never a feature of the world—it was a feature of a particular era. That era is over. Accepting this is not pessimism; it is the beginning of genuine adaptability.

- Organisations eliminate roles, not talent. When a role disappears, the capabilities that filled it do not. The professional who understands this recovers faster and more purposefully.

- The half-life of skills is shrinking. Learning is no longer something you do at the start of a career. It is the career.

- The individual, not the institution, is the constant. Professional identity must be anchored in personal capability—not in a title, a company, or a role that may not exist in five years.

The chapters that follow move from diagnosis to design. Having understood why permanence has faded, we can begin to build something more durable in its place—not a new set of guarantees, but a new kind of readiness.

REFLECT ON THIS

1. Is there a role, organisation, or professional identity you are still holding onto longer than is wise? What would it take to release it—and what might become possible if you did?

2. If your current role disappeared tomorrow, what capabilities would you carry forward? Are those capabilities sufficient—or is there a gap you have been avoiding?

3. Think of someone you admire professionally who has navigated significant change with grace. What did they do that you have not yet done?

PART 2

The Central Idea – You INC.

CHAPTER 4

Reimagining Yourself as a Corporation

The first three chapters of this book have been, in a sense, about the terrain. The disappearance of predictable careers. The acceleration of disruption. The fading of permanence. If you have been reading with a slightly uncomfortable sense of recognition, that is entirely the point.

But a diagnosis without a direction is merely anxiety with footnotes. The question a young woman in the front row put to me at the end of a long session at a business school was exactly the right one—and it is the question this section of the book tries to answer.

> *It came at the end of a long afternoon session at a business school, after I had spent the better part of two hours talking about leadership, disruption, and the changing nature of careers. Most of the students had begun packing up their bags. A few were already texting furiously. And then a young woman in the front row, who had been quiet throughout the entire session, raised her hand.*
>
> *"Sir," she said, "you've told us what the world looks like. But what exactly are we supposed to do about it?"*

> *The room settled again. It was a fair challenge. I had spent two hours describing the terrain and not nearly enough time on the question of navigation.*
>
> *I thought for a moment before answering.*
>
> *"Start by thinking of yourself differently," I said. "Not as a person looking for a role. But as an enterprise looking to create value."*
>
> *She frowned slightly. "You mean like a startup?"*
>
> *"Closer than you think," I told her. "But simpler. I mean like a corporation. A small one, run entirely by you, with you as its only irreplaceable asset."*

That idea, simple as it sounds, is the hinge on which everything in this section of the book turns.

A Different Way of Seeing Yourself

For most of our professional lives, we see ourselves as participants in systems that others have built. We join organisations. We perform roles. We climb, or occasionally slide down, ladders that someone else constructed. There is nothing wrong with this. Organisations create real opportunities. Institutions offer structure, community, and resources that individuals cannot easily replicate on their own.

But the world we discussed in the first three chapters of this book has complicated that picture considerably. When industries transform every few years, when automation steadily reshapes the nature of work, and when the relationship between employer and employee grows increasingly transactional, waiting for an organisation to manage your development becomes a risky strategy.

"The past has no future. The career frameworks of the past were built on assumptions about permanence that no longer hold. If you rely entirely on an institution to define, develop, and protect your professional life, you are building your house on someone else's land."

Which brings me back to the young woman in the front row. Her name was Zara. She had introduced herself briefly at the start of the session—second-year student, part-time content creator, clearly someone who thought harder about things than she let on. After the session ended, she came up to the front as the others filed out.

> *"Sir, I liked the idea," she said, "but I want to push back a little."*
>
> *"Please do," I said.*
>
> *"You said think like a corporation. But corporations are often the problem, aren't they? The ones laying people off, restructuring on a whim, discarding people after twenty years of service."*
>
> *It was a sharp observation, and she deserved a straight answer.*
>
> *"You're right," I said. "Some corporations behave very badly. But that's not what I'm asking you to emulate. I'm asking you to borrow their discipline, not their callousness. The way a good corporation thinks about its own survival, capabilities, and long-term relevance. That part is worth copying."*

> *She considered this. "So it's more about the mindset than the model?"*
>
> *"Exactly that," I said.*
>
> *She nodded slowly, the way people do when an idea hasn't quite settled but they can see where it's heading.*

What Corporations Actually Do

Before the idea can be useful, it is worth being precise about what it means. A corporation, stripped of its complexity, is a system designed to create value over time. It identifies what it is genuinely good at. It builds the capabilities required to deliver that value. It manages its resources carefully. It invests in relationships that expand its reach. And it constantly asks whether it is still relevant to the world it operates in.

When I describe it that way to audiences, people often smile with a flicker of recognition. Because individuals do all of these things too. We build skills. We form professional networks. We make decisions about where to invest our time and energy. We assess whether our current situation is moving us toward where we want to go.

The difference is not in the activity. It is in the intentionality. Organisations think about these things deliberately, systematically, and with a long-term horizon. Most individuals think about them only when circumstances force the question—which is usually when something has already gone wrong.

I think here of Vikram. We had met after a leadership workshop, and he sat across from me with the quiet exhaustion of a man who had done everything right and was only now beginning to wonder whether that was enough.

"Five years ago we were the market leaders," he had said. "What changed?" I asked. He paused for a long moment. "I think we confused being good at what we did with being prepared for what was coming." He was talking about his company. But the sentence applied equally to himself. He was talented, experienced, and—for the first time in his career—genuinely uncertain about whether those things would be sufficient. That is the precise moment when thinking like a corporation becomes essential.

Your Capabilities Are Your Product Line

Every corporation has a product portfolio. Some products are mature and reliable. Others are new and still being tested. A few are in decline and need to be retired before they drain too many resources. Your capabilities work in exactly the same way.

Some of what you know today is dependable and in demand. Some of it is emerging and needs further investment. And some of it—though this is rarely comfortable to acknowledge—is quietly losing relevance in a world that is moving quickly past it. I have said this to senior professionals over many years, and it never quite lands easily. The natural instinct is to treat accumulated experience as an unqualified asset, something that simply grows more valuable with time.

> **"Experience is baggage. The market does not value it; what the market values is relevance. If you stopped learning five years ago, you are not five years experienced—you are five years out of date."**

This is not meant to dismiss the genuine wisdom that experience carries. It is meant to challenge the assumption that experience alone is sufficient. Vikram, to his credit, understood this when I put it to him. "I've been living off a reputation I built a decade ago," he said. "I haven't been adding to it. I've been spending it." That is a very honest thing for a senior executive to say. And it is, in my experience, more common than most people at that level are willing to admit.

The corporate mindset asks a harder question: what are you building today that will be valuable tomorrow?

Your Network Is Your Ecosystem

No corporation of any significance operates in isolation. Even the most powerful companies in the world maintain extensive networks of partners, suppliers, collaborators, and customers. These relationships form ecosystems that allow organisations to reach further, learn faster, and respond more effectively to change than they ever could alone. Individuals have equivalent ecosystems. We call them networks, though that word has acquired a slightly transactional ring that does not quite capture what the best professional relationships actually are.

The relationships that matter most in a career are rarely purely instrumental. They tend to be built on genuine curiosity, shared experiences, and mutual generosity. The mentor who gave you time when you did not yet deserve it. The colleague who recommended you for something before you would have recommended yourself. The chance conversation at an unremarkable conference that eventually changed the direction of your thinking.

Aarav told me after one session that he found networking uncomfortable. "I never know what I am supposed to be getting from it," he said. "That is because you are thinking about what to extract," I replied. "Think instead about what you can offer. The ecosystem rewards generosity more reliably than strategy." He thought about this. "So it is less like a transaction and more like a garden?" "Exactly like a garden," I said. "You tend it regularly, without always knowing which plant will eventually bear fruit. And you never go in asking which flower owes you something." He laughed. But the image, I think, stayed with him.

The Question of Strategy

Once you begin to see yourself through this lens, a natural question follows. If you are an enterprise with capabilities, relationships, and accumulated experience, what is the strategy that ties it all together? In a corporate context, strategy simply means having a view about where you are going and making deliberate choices that move you in that direction. It does not require certainty. It does not demand a five-year plan written in triplicate. It asks only that you are paying attention to the direction in which your decisions are pointing.

Which opportunity develops a capability you will need? Which role exposes you to a context you do not yet understand? Which relationship, if invested in now, might matter more than you can currently calculate?

I once had a conversation with Arjun, who had resigned from a well-regarded corporate career to start a boutique consulting firm. Eighteen months in, the enterprise was surviving—just about. He told me he had left his company because he wanted freedom. "And do you have it?" I asked. A long pause. "I have something," he said. "I'm not sure freedom is the right word for it." "What word would you use?" He thought for a moment. "Exposure. I am exposed in ways I wasn't before. I have to sell, which I never had to do. I have to manage client anxiety, which I was insulated from. I have to decide everything, which sounds appealing until you realise how much mental energy decisions consume." "Do you regret it?" "No," he said. "But I wish I had thought about where I was going, rather than just where I was leaving from." That distinction—moving toward something rather than simply away from something—is one of the most important ideas in this book. The YOU INC. mindset is not a philosophy of escape. It is a philosophy of design.

The Permanent Beta State

There is one more corporate principle that I believe matters above all others for individuals navigating the modern world. The most resilient organisations share a particular quality. They never fully believe that they have arrived. Regardless of their current success, they continue experimenting, questioning their assumptions, and testing new approaches.

> **"It's important to remain in a permanent beta state and never becoming a finished product because a finished product might finish you."**

This principle is, I think, the most important one in this entire book. The professionals who remain vital and relevant across long careers are not necessarily the most talented or the most credentialled. They are the ones who never stopped being curious. Who allowed their thinking to be challenged and revised. Who treated each new chapter of their career as an opportunity to become a slightly better version of the enterprise they were running.

I said something like this to Shoma one evening, after a long day that had involved one too many conversations with people who were entirely certain they already knew everything worth knowing. "The dangerous ones are the finished products," I told her. "The ones who have stopped questioning themselves." She looked up from her book. "That is true," she said. "Though I notice you have been saying the same things for 20 years." I laughed. She was not entirely wrong. Some ideas, tested over time, earn the right to be repeated. The trick is knowing which ones—and remaining genuinely open to being surprised by the rest.

The Enterprise Called You

The chapters that follow in this section will explore each dimension of the YOU INC. idea in greater detail: how to build personal infrastructure, how to manage your capabilities deliberately, and how to develop the inner resilience that sustains a career across multiple reinventions. But it begins here, with a simple shift in perspective.

You are not simply an employee, a professional, or a job title. You are an evolving enterprise with a unique combination of experience, capability, and relationships. That enterprise needs to be led with the same seriousness, curiosity, and long-term thinking that any well-run organisation brings to its own development. The world we described in Part One of this book is not going to become simpler or more forgiving. But individuals who have made the shift described in this chapter, who have accepted genuine responsibility for their own growth, navigate that world from a fundamentally different position. They are not waiting to be managed. They are managing themselves. And that, in an unpredictable world, turns out to be a very considerable advantage.

KEY TAKEAWAYS

- Thinking of yourself as a corporation is not metaphor—it is method. It shifts your relationship with your own development from passive to deliberate.
- Your capabilities are your product line. Some are growing, some are mature, some are quietly becoming obsolete. Delineating them is the beginning of genuine strategy.
- Your network is an ecosystem, not a contact list. It grows through generosity and genuine curiosity—not through extraction or transactional thinking.

- The permanent beta state is not restlessness. It is the disciplined refusal to believe you are finished—and the commitment to keep building regardless of current success.

The YOU INC. framework is not a formula. It is a way of seeing. Once you begin to look at your professional life through this lens—as an enterprise with a product line, an ecosystem, a strategy, and a permanent commitment to evolution—the questions you ask about your career change entirely. And better questions tend to produce better answers.

REFLECT ON THIS

1. If your capabilities were a product portfolio, which would you classify as growing, which as mature, and which as quietly declining? Be honest.

2. Think of the three relationships that have mattered most in your career. What made them powerful—and are you investing in relationships of similar quality today?

3. Where in your professional life are you behaving like a finished product—certain, settled, no longer questioning? What would it take to re-enter beta?

CHAPTER 5

Corporatising the Self

Over the years, I have shared the YOU INC. idea with a great many people—in classrooms, boardrooms, over dinners, and occasionally on long flights when the person in the next seat made the mistake of asking what I did for a living. The reactions vary. Some people find it immediately energising. Others are intrigued but unsure how to begin. A few push back, which I always find more interesting than easy agreement.

But the response that has stayed with me most vividly came from a friend who works in finance. Precise by temperament, methodical by training, and deeply allergic to anything that smells of vague aspiration. If you tell him you are planning to "work on yourself," he will smile politely and change the subject. So, when we met for lunch, I was curious how much of the YOU INC. idea he would find useful—and how much he would find too soft for his taste.

> *What I did not know, until that lunch, was that he had heard me speak about this idea once before—years earlier, at an industry conference where I had given a talk about individuals thinking of themselves as enterprises. He had been in the audience. He mentioned it almost in passing, the way people do when they assume you remember every speech you have ever given.*
>
> *I did not remember it. But he did.*

He reached into his bag and slid a notebook across the table.

At the top of the open page, written in his characteristically neat hand, were three words: Me Inc. Review.

Below it was a set of questions laid out in sections. What worked this year. What did not. Capabilities developed. Relationships invested in. Plans for the year ahead.

"You do this every year?" I asked.

"Every January," he said. "Without fail. I started the year after that conference. So—eleven years now."

"And it helps?"

He gave me a look that suggested he found the question slightly beneath both of us. "If companies need to review themselves to keep improving," he said, "why on earth would I not?"

I was pleased, and I told him so. Not because he had validated my thinking—though that was gratifying—but because he had done something more useful. He had taken an idea from a conference hall, carried it home, and quietly built it into the architecture of his professional life. He had translated a philosophical idea into a practical habit. He had built the plumbing. And he had been running it, without fanfare, for over a decade.

That, in essence, is what this chapter is about. Chapter 4 introduced the idea of thinking of yourself as a corporation. This chapter is about what that looks like in practice. Not the philosophy, but the plumbing.

The Gap between Intention and Action

Most professionals I have met over the course of my career are genuinely well-intentioned about their own development. They mean to sharpen their skills. They intend to build deeper networks. They plan to reflect more carefully on where their careers are heading. These are not empty sentiments. The intentions are real.

The problem is that intentions, left to themselves, are extremely unreliable. Daily work has an extraordinary capacity to fill every available hour. Meetings accumulate, deadlines arrive, and the urgent steadily crowds out the important. Months pass with remarkable speed. And the things we intended to do quietly wait in the background, still waiting, with the mild reproach of the perpetually deferred.

Corporations encounter exactly the same problem. Left to their own momentum, organisations tend to repeat yesterday's activities rather than invest in tomorrow's capabilities. This is why well-run companies do not rely on good intentions. They build systems. Corporatising the self is essentially the same idea applied to an individual life. It means introducing a small number of deliberate practices that ensure the important work of your own development does not get perpetually deferred. Not rigid procedures. Not a bureaucracy of one. Just enough structure to make progress possible.

Starting with Purpose

Every company worth studying has, at its heart, a reason for existing that goes beyond the immediate business at hand. Call it purpose, mission, or strategic intent—the label matters less than the function. It provides direction. It makes certain decisions easier and others obviously unnecessary. Individuals rarely pause to articulate something equivalent.

I once asked a group of mid-career professionals a question that I thought was straightforward: *what kind of work do you want to become known for? Not what role do you currently hold, or what company you work for, but what is the contribution you hope to make over time?* The room went very quiet. Far quieter than I expected. It turned out the question was not straightforward at all. Most people are entirely comfortable describing their current situation. The future-facing version of the same question is considerably harder.

Meera came to mind when I reflected on that silence afterwards. I had met her through a mutual contact—she was in the process of returning to the workforce after a four-year break, and she was finding the re-entry considerably more disorienting than she had anticipated. We met for coffee, and she arrived with a carefully updated CV and an expression that combined determination with something she was working hard not to show.

> *"I know what I have done," she said, placing the CV on the table between us. "What I am struggling with is how to say what I want to do next."*
>
> *"Start by forgetting the CV for a moment," I said.*
>
> *She looked at me with polite suspicion. "I spent three weeks on that."*
>
> *"I know. And we will come back to it. But tell me first—not what you are qualified for. What kind of problems do you find genuinely interesting? What does good work feel like for you, when it is actually good?"*

She was quiet for a moment. Then, slowly, she began to talk. Not about her previous titles or her reporting lines, but about the campaigns she had built that she was proud of. The teams she had developed. The moments when she had walked out of a meeting feeling that something had shifted in the right direction.

By the time the coffee was cold, she had said far more interesting things than anything on her CV.

"That," I told her, "is your purpose. Not a job description. That feeling, and the work that produces it."

She looked at the CV lying between us. "So, what do I do with this?"

"Now you rewrite it," I said. "But from the inside out, rather than the outside in."

Purpose, in this sense, does not need to be elaborate or grand. It might simply be a statement about the kind of problems you find genuinely interesting, the values you want your work to express, or the area of expertise you are building toward. It does not need to last a lifetime. It simply needs to exist. Because without some sense of direction, every opportunity looks equally attractive, and every distraction carries equal weight.

"Start with a sense of who you want to become and then ask what today's choices need to look like in order to support that trajectory."

Turning Intentions into Goals

Purpose provides the direction. Goals provide the movement. Organisations do not run on aspiration alone. They translate their ambitions into targets that are specific enough to be pursued and concrete enough to be measured. This discipline forces a kind of honesty that vague intentions never require.

Individuals tend to stop one step short of this. We tell ourselves we should improve a particular skill, or invest more time in a relationship, or make progress on a long-deferred project. And then we watch, with a mixture of guilt and mild bewilderment, as the year passes and none of it has happened. The remedy is specificity. Not "I should improve my writing" but "I will spend forty-five minutes on Thursday mornings putting thoughts on paper." Not "I should reconnect with old colleagues" but "I will reach out to two people I have lost touch with each month." The content of the goal matters less than its precision. Precision creates accountability.

I once asked Aarav, during a follow-up conversation after one of my sessions, what his goals were for the coming year. He pulled out his phone immediately. "I have a list," he said. It was a long list—impressively long, in fact—17 items, organised under three broad headings. "That is ambitious," I said. He grinned. "I believe in thinking big." "I believe in thinking precisely," I said. "Choose three. Not seventeen. Three things that, if you accomplish them by December, will make a genuine difference to where you are headed. And for each one, write down not just what you want to achieve, but how you will know you have achieved it." He looked slightly deflated. "Only three?" "Start with three. If you finish them, you will know exactly what to add next. A list of 17 is an aspiration. A list of three, pursued seriously, is a plan." He thought about it. Then he put the phone away and asked for a pen. That, I thought, was a good sign.

"Victory loves preparation."

The Annual Review You Never Had

One of the practices I have long encouraged—and which my finance friend had arrived at independently, with his customary precision—is the personal annual review. Organisations periodically pause to take stock. They examine what has been accomplished, identify where progress stalled, and decide what deserves attention next. Done honestly, this is not a judgment exercise. It is a learning exercise. Individuals rarely do this for themselves.

Years flow by in a continuous stream of activity, and the deeper question—*what have I actually learned from all of this*—mostly goes unasked. Experiences accumulate, but the lessons embedded in them often go unexamined. I have done a version of this myself for many years, with considerably less neatness and somewhat more coffee than my friend would probably approve of. But even in an informal form, the practice reveals things that are genuinely surprising. A project that felt unremarkable at the time turns out to have developed a capability I did not notice gaining. A relationship I neglected shows up in the review as a quiet gap. A commitment I made with great confidence at the start of the year sits there at the end, untouched, asking a question I cannot easily ignore.

Arjun told me that before he left his corporate role, he had not once sat down to review his own year in this way. Performance reviews happened, of course—but those were other people's assessments of his work, filtered through institutional metrics that did not always capture what mattered. "I never asked myself what I had actually learned," he said. "I just moved from one year to the next, assuming I was growing because my title was changing." "And were you growing?" He was quiet for a moment. "In some ways. But looking back, I was also repeating myself. Doing the same things with greater confidence, but not necessarily with greater wisdom." That distinction—between accumulated confidence and accumulated wisdom—is one worth sitting with.

Protecting Your Most Valuable Resources

Every corporation manages its capital carefully. Financial resources are allocated, monitored, and evaluated for the returns they generate. No serious organisation allows its most valuable assets to be spent thoughtlessly. Individuals have equivalent resources. They are simply less visible and therefore far easier to squander. Time. Energy. Attention. These three, in combination, constitute the working capital of a personal enterprise. And they are finite in ways that feel abstract until you notice, sometime in your forties, that you are tired in ways that an early night no longer fully resolves.

> **"It is important to focus on the next shot."**

This discipline—directing your most valuable resources toward what matters most, rather than allowing them to be drained by whatever is immediately demanding—is one of the most underrated practices in professional life. Busyness is not the same as productivity. Activity is not the same as progress.

Shoma said something to me during a period when I was particularly scattered across too many commitments, that I found difficult to argue with. "You are everywhere," she said, "and therefore nowhere." It was not intended as a compliment. But it was an accurate description of what happens when personal capital is spread too thin. I had said yes to too many things, attended too many meetings that needed my presence only in the most nominal sense, and allowed the important work to accumulate while the urgent work consumed every available hour. The correction, when I finally made it, was less dramatic than it sounds. I simply became more willing to say no—and more deliberate about which yeses deserved my best energy rather than whatever was left at the end of an already full day.

Meera understood this intuitively, perhaps because her four-year break had given her a clarity about time that most people only acquire the hard way. When I asked her how she was thinking about her re-entry, she said something that struck me as genuinely wise. "I am not going to try to make up for lost time," she said. "I do not think that is how time works. I am going to be very careful about what I spend it on from here." That, in essence, is what managing your working capital looks like in practice.

Systems Over Willpower

Corporations do not run on motivation. They run on systems. Processes, rhythms, and routines ensure that important work happens consistently, regardless of whether anyone feels particularly inspired on a given Tuesday morning. The weekly meeting happens because it is scheduled, not because everyone arrived at the office feeling enthusiastic about it. Individuals tend to rely on willpower instead. We intend to exercise regularly, read more widely, invest time in learning. And these intentions hold up reasonably well when life is orderly. But when schedules become dense and energy runs low, willpower is usually the first casualty. Systems survive where willpower fails.

A simple weekly review—thirty minutes at the end of the week to look back at what happened and plan what comes next—creates a rhythm that reactive scheduling never provides. *A regular reading habit,* however modest, accumulates into a meaningful body of knowledge over years. *A standing conversation with a mentor,* however infrequent, creates a relationship that provides perspective precisely when it is needed. None of these require exceptional discipline. They require only that they are treated as non-negotiable rather than aspirational.

"Consistency is a better virtue."

The professionals I have most admired over a long career were rarely the most dramatically gifted. They were the ones who showed up prepared, every time, without the need for a special occasion to justify it. That consistency, sustained over years, produces a kind of compound effect that occasional brilliance rarely matches.

I think of Naren in this regard. He had built one of the most distinguished corporate careers of his generation—decades of leadership, a reputation that preceded him into every room he entered. When I asked him once what he considered his most important professional habit, I expected something strategic, perhaps something about decision-making or managing people under pressure. "Reading," he said, without hesitation. "Every day. Without exception. Not industry reports. Books. History, philosophy, biography, the occasional novel. I have done it since I was in my twenties." "Even during the busiest periods?" "Especially during the busiest periods," he said. "Thirty minutes in the morning before anything else. It is non-negotiable. Not because I always find something useful in what I read, but because the habit keeps me from becoming entirely absorbed in the immediate. It reminds me that the world is larger than my current problem." A system, not a resolution. Thirty minutes a day, every day, for decades. The compound interest on that investment is incalculable.

The Role of Accountability

Well-run organisations do not make important decisions in a vacuum. Boards provide oversight. Mentors offer perspective. Trusted advisors ask the questions that internal enthusiasm sometimes crowds out. These structures exist not to restrict autonomy but to improve judgement. Even the most experienced leaders benefit from having someone in their professional life who will say, with genuine care, "Are you sure about this?" Individuals often operate without anything comparable.

Aarav told me once that he found it difficult to ask for guidance.

"It feels like admitting I do not know what I am doing," he said.

"That is precisely the point," I told him. "Nobody fully knows what they are doing. The ones who seek perspective simply end up making better decisions than the ones who pretend otherwise."

He thought about this. "So, asking for help is not a weakness."

"It is the opposite," I said. "It is the most honest thing an intelligent person can do."

My finance friend reviews his notebook with his wife every January. Not because she manages his career, but because having a witness to the process makes the process real in a way it would not be otherwise. The act of explaining your intentions to another person forces a clarity that thinking alone rarely produces.

Running the Enterprise Called You

None of what this chapter describes is complicated. A clear sense of purpose. Goals with enough specificity to be pursued. Periodic reviews that transform experience into learning. Protection of your most valuable resources. Systems that create consistency where willpower would eventually fail. And some form of accountability that keeps the whole enterprise honest. Taken individually, these practices are modest. Taken together, sustained over time, they constitute a fundamentally different relationship with your own professional development. The corporation of you begins to run deliberately rather than accidentally. Progress stops being something that happens when circumstances cooperate, and starts being something that is, at least in part, designed.

The annual review, the precise goal, the protected hour on Thursday mornings—these are not ends in themselves. They are the mechanisms through which a person remains genuinely open to growth. They make the permanent beta state possible in practice, rather than merely admirable in theory.

My friend's notebook was not, in the end, a curiosity. It was evidence of a particular kind of seriousness about one's own life. Not the performative seriousness of the person who talks endlessly about self-improvement while never quite getting around to any of it. The quieter, more durable kind. The kind that shows up in January with a pen and a notebook and asks, without drama or fanfare, what needs to be different this year. That question, asked honestly and regularly, turns out to be one of the more powerful things a person can do.

KEY TAKEAWAYS

- Good intentions are not a system. The gap between what we mean to do and what we actually do is almost always a structural problem—and structural problems require structural solutions.
- Purpose is not a grand statement. It is simply a clear enough sense of direction that some choices become easier and others obviously unnecessary.
- The annual review is one of the most valuable practices available to a professional—and one of the least used. Done honestly, it transforms experience into learning rather than just letting it pass.
- Consistency compounds. The professional who shows up prepared, every time, quietly outperforms the one who relies on occasional bursts of brilliance.

Corporatising the self is not about becoming robotic or overly structured. It is about taking your own development seriously enough to give it the same attention you would give to any enterprise worth running well. The notebook, the goal, the weekly review—these are not ends in themselves. They are how the permanent beta state becomes real in practice, rather than merely admirable in theory.

REFLECT ON THIS

1. If you conducted a Me Inc. Review today, what would the honest answers reveal? What developed this year—and what has been quietly waiting on the list for longer than you care to admit?

2. What is the single most important investment you could make in your own development right now? What system—not intention, but system—would ensure it actually happens?

3. Who in your life serves as a genuine accountability partner for your professional development? If no one does, what would it take to change that?

CHAPTER 6

Building Personal Infrastructure

There is a stretch of road not far from where I grew up in Kolkata that I have passed hundreds of times over the years. For most of my childhood it was unremarkable—narrow, uneven, flanked by the particular kind of organised chaos that Kolkata does better than anywhere else on earth.

Then one year, for months, it was completely impassable. Pipes were being laid underground. Cables were being rerouted. The surface was torn up entirely. It looked, for a long while, considerably worse than it had before the work began. When it reopened, nothing appeared dramatically different. The road looked more or less like a road. Pedestrians walked on it. Vehicles drove along it. To a passing observer, not much seemed to have changed. But beneath the surface, everything had changed. The infrastructure that would support everything above it for the next several decades had been quietly put in place.

I have thought about that road often when reflecting on what makes certain professionals genuinely durable over long careers. The ones who remain effective and relevant across very different circumstances are rarely the ones who made the most noise or accumulated the most impressive titles in their early years. They are the ones who spent time building something beneath the surface that most people never see. They built infrastructure.

The Invisible Architecture of a Career

When we observe someone handling a complex situation with apparent ease—navigating a difficult negotiation, reframing a problem that had everyone else stuck, moving into an unfamiliar role and finding their footing quickly—we tend to explain it as talent, or experience, or confidence. Sometimes it is all of those things. But more often, what we are observing is the product of capabilities built quietly over time, mostly out of public view.

> *Early in my career, there was a senior colleague whose reputation preceded him into every room he entered. Not because he was the most visible person in the organisation, or the most vocal in meetings. Quite the opposite. He had a quality of stillness that I found, initially, slightly puzzling. When a project hit trouble—and in the organisations I worked in, projects hit trouble with reliable frequency—someone would inevitably say, "Has anyone spoken to him?"*
>
> *He did not always have immediate answers. He would listen, ask a few careful questions, and then say something I came to recognise as one of the more honest things a senior person can say: "Give me a day to think about it."*
>
> *The following morning he would return, and what he offered was rarely flashy. It was thorough. It was grounded. And it almost always pointed toward something that had not been considered.*
>
> *I asked him once, during a quiet moment, how he approached problems that nobody else seemed able to crack.*
>
> *He smiled in the way people do when they find a question unexpectedly simple. "I have spent years learning how to think," he said. "Not about this industry specifically. About problems in general."*

That answer has stayed with me for decades. Because what he was describing was not expertise. It was infrastructure. The underlying capacity to engage with unfamiliar situations and find a way through them—built through years of deliberate and wide-ranging intellectual investment.

What Personal Infrastructure Actually Means

In a corporate context, infrastructure refers to the capabilities, systems, and foundations that make everything else possible. The product the customer sees is, in a sense, just the tip of the iceberg. Beneath it lies the engineering, the processes, the knowledge, and the institutional capability that allows it to exist at all. Personal infrastructure works in the same way. The visible outputs of a professional life—the project delivered, the role performed, the problem solved—rest on a foundation of capabilities that are far less visible but far more determinative of long-term success.

The most important of these are not technical skills in any narrow sense. Technical skills matter, and they need to be kept current. But the deeper infrastructure consists of capacities that transcend any particular role or industry. The ability to learn quickly. The capacity to adapt when circumstances shift unexpectedly. Resilience in the face of setbacks. The habit of thinking across disciplines rather than within them. And the particular quality, rarer than it should be, of being genuinely curious about how things work.

> **"Ignorance is supreme knowledge. The professional who approaches unfamiliar territory with genuine curiosity—who is comfortable not knowing, and is energised by the prospect of finding out—has a profound advantage over one who must always appear to already have the answer.**

Vikram understood this, though it took him longer than he would have liked to admit it. I met him again some months after our first conversation, and he seemed different—less armoured, somehow. He told me he had started attending a weekly session run by a group of entrepreneurs, most of them considerably younger than him. "I am usually the oldest person in the room by about fifteen years," he said. "And how is that?" "Uncomfortable," he said. "Which I have decided is the point." He had stopped needing to be the most knowledgeable person present. And in doing so, he had started learning again in a way he had not for years. That shift—from performing expertise to building it—is one of the most important moves a mid-career professional can make.

Learning as a Lifelong Discipline

Of all the elements that constitute personal infrastructure, the ability and habit of continuous learning is probably the most important. I want to be careful here, because the word "learning" has acquired a slightly exhausting quality in professional discourse. It has become associated with online courses, certification programmes, and the obligation to be perpetually upskilling in ways that can feel more anxious than enriching. That is not what I mean. What I mean is the quieter discipline of staying genuinely curious. Of reading books that have nothing to do with your current job. Of having conversations that take you into territory you do not already occupy. Of asking, with real interest, how other fields approach the problems yours is currently struggling with.

> *A former student of mine, someone I have stayed in touch with over many years, told me about a personal practice he had maintained since his late twenties. Every year, he said, he deliberately learned one thing that made him uncomfortable.*

> *One year it was public speaking, which he had avoided for most of his career with considerable ingenuity. Another year it was basic data analytics, which he approached with the trepidation of someone who had confidently identified himself as "not a numbers person" for the previous decade. More recently, he said, it was writing—the sustained kind, where you have to organise your thoughts rather than simply deliver them in conversation.*
>
> *None of these efforts produced immediate career results. But over time, he told me, he had noticed something. He was comfortable in situations that his peers found unsettling. He could have conversations across functions that others found difficult. And he had, without quite planning for it, become the kind of person who was useful in a broader range of circumstances.*

"If one already knows the answer, the question is probably wrong. This habit of deliberately exposing oneself to unfamiliar perspectives trains the mind to hold multiple frameworks simultaneously."

The Case for Cross-Disciplinary Thinking

The most interesting conversations I have had over a long career have rarely stayed within a single domain. The best ones wander. They begin in one field and find their way, through a series of unexpected connections, into another. Someone draws on a reference from history to illuminate a problem in marketing. Someone else applies an insight from behavioural science to a question about organisational design. A third person, who studied engineering before moving into general management, asks a structural question that reframes everything. These moments of intellectual cross-pollination are not accidental. They happen because certain people have invested, over years, in building a mind that does not stay neatly within its professional lane.

Zara had this quality naturally, though she did not quite recognise it as a strength yet. She had built her content creation practice by instinctively borrowing from journalism, psychology, and design—disciplines she had never formally studied but had absorbed through relentless curiosity. When I pointed this out to her, she looked mildly surprised. "I just read a lot of things that interest me," she said. "That is precisely the habit," I told her. "Most people read only what their job requires. You read what your mind requires. Over time, the difference is enormous." She thought about this. "So it is not wasted time." "It is the opposite of wasted time. It is compound interest on curiosity."

Cross-disciplinary thinking does not require formal breadth—two degrees, three industries, a decade abroad. It requires only curiosity and the willingness to read, listen, and engage beyond the immediate demands of one's current role. Over time, the connections accumulate. The intellectual range expands. And the infrastructure becomes richer for it.

Resilience Is Not a Personality Trait

Resilience tends to be discussed as though it were something you either have or you do not—a temperamental feature that some people are lucky enough to be born with, and others simply have to manage without. I do not believe that. I think resilience is, in large part, infrastructure. It is built through the accumulation of experiences navigated, setbacks absorbed, and lessons extracted from both. The professional who has been through difficult periods and come out the other side carrying something useful from the experience is not just tougher. They are better equipped. They know, from direct personal evidence, that they can get through things. That knowledge changes how you carry yourself when the next difficulty arrives.

Arjun described this to me during one of our conversations, about a year into his consulting venture. The early anxiety had not disappeared, he said, but it had changed in quality. "In the beginning," he told me, “Every slow month felt like evidence that I had made a terrible mistake. Now it just feels like a slow month." "What changed?" I asked. "I have been through enough of them to know they end," he said. "That sounds obvious. But you don't actually know it until you have lived it a few times." That is resilience built from experience, not temperament. He had not become a different person. He had simply accumulated enough evidence to trust himself—and that trust had become part of his infrastructure.

Meera had something similar, though her evidence had been gathered in a very different arena. Four years of managing a family through illness, keeping herself intellectually alive through reading and mentoring, holding together a life that required her full presence every single day—none of this appeared on her CV. But all of it had added, quietly and without fanfare, to the infrastructure she was carrying forward. "The break cost me professionally," she said to me once, with characteristic directness. "I am not pretending otherwise. But it also built things in me that I could not have built any other way." I believed her completely.

Building It Steadily

Infrastructure is not built in a single dramatic effort. It is accumulated, gradually, through small and consistent investments that rarely feel significant in the moment. Reading widely. Maintaining the habit of reflection. Seeking out conversations with people who think differently. Saying yes, occasionally, to the unfamiliar assignment that no one else is particularly eager to take on. Extracting, deliberately, the lesson from each experience rather than simply moving on to the next one.

None of these activities produces a headline result. You will not be promoted because you spent a year developing genuine intellectual curiosity, or because you read books outside your professional discipline, or because you allowed a difficult period to teach you something rather than simply enduring it. But over time, the compound effect becomes visible. Not as a single achievement, but as a quality of presence—the kind of person who is genuinely useful in a wide range of situations, who moves through uncertainty with something that resembles groundedness, and who continues to evolve when those around them have quietly stopped.

> **"Purpose in a pursuit is the source of energy and timelessness."**

The professional who is genuinely building something—not just performing a role but developing as a person—brings a different quality of energy to their work. I have seen it many times, and it is unmistakable. There is a quality of aliveness in people who are still growing that no title or salary can replicate. The infrastructure and the purpose reinforce each other. The deeper the foundations, the further the range of meaningful activity they support.

Naren said something to me during one of our conversations that I have thought about many times since. He was reflecting on the long arc of his career—the decades of building, leading, deciding—and I asked him what he wished he had understood earlier. He did not hesitate. "That the work you do on yourself is never separate from the work you do in the world," he said. "I used to think of personal development as something you did before the real work began. I now think it is the real work. Everything else is an expression of it." Coming from someone who had led organisations for 30 years, that was not a small thing to say.

The Road Beneath the Road

When the work on that road in Kolkata was finally complete and the surface was restored, most people simply walked on it again without a second thought. The pipes and cables and foundations laid beneath were entirely invisible. They did exactly what good infrastructure is supposed to do: function reliably and without fanfare. The same is largely true of personal infrastructure. No one will gather to applaud the intellectual range you quietly built over a decade of curious reading. No one will notice, at first, the resilience you developed by extracting lessons from experiences that most people simply endured and moved past. But it will be there. Supporting everything you do. Enabling you to go further, adapt more fluidly, and remain genuinely relevant across circumstances that cannot yet be predicted.

KEY TAKEAWAYS

- The most durable professional asset is not expertise—it is the capacity to engage with unfamiliar problems and find a way through them. That capacity is infrastructure, and it is built over years, mostly out of public view.
- Continuous learning does not mean perpetual upskilling. It means staying genuinely curious—reading beyond your field, seeking perspectives that unsettle your assumptions, remaining a student of the world.
- Resilience is not a personality trait. It is built experience by experience, setback by setback, each time you extract the lesson rather than simply enduring the moment.

- Infrastructure compounds quietly. The intellectual range, the cross-disciplinary connections, the inner steadiness—none of these announce themselves dramatically. But over time, they become the foundation that holds everything else up.

Chapters 4 and 5 explored the operational side of thinking like a corporation—the purpose, the goals, the reviews, and the systems. This chapter has been about something deeper: the foundation beneath the structure. Build the infrastructure. The rest of the enterprise will have something solid to stand on.

REFLECT ON THIS

1. Think of a professional you admire who handles uncertainty with apparent ease. What have they built, over time, that you have not yet built? Is that a gap you are willing to close?

2. What is the last book you read that had nothing to do with your current job? What did it open up—and when did you last deliberately seek out that kind of intellectual discomfort?

3. Think of a setback you have experienced in the past few years. Did you extract the lesson from it—or did you simply move on? What would extracting that lesson actually require?

YOU INC. – A MID-POINT AUDIT

Parts 1 & 2

The World Has Changed

– The Central Idea –

You are now halfway through this book. Before moving into Part 3, it is worth pausing—not to test what you remember, but to examine what you actually think. The questions below are not a quiz. There are no correct answers. They are the kind of questions a well-run corporation would ask of itself at the mid-year mark. You are the corporation. This is your review.

Find a quiet moment. Answer honestly. The value is not in getting it right—it is in the quality of your attention to yourself.

THE WORLD YOU ARE IN

Which of the disruptions described in Part 1 feels most personally relevant to your own career right now? What are you doing about it?

What assumption about your career or industry have you been carrying longest? Is it still reliable—or has it quietly stopped being true?

YOUR CAPABILITIES

If your capabilities were a product portfolio, which would you honestly classify as growing, which as mature, and which as quietly becoming obsolete?

What is one skill or capability you have been meaning to build for two years or more? What has actually stopped you?

YOUR STRATEGY

Are you managing your present from your future—or your future from your present? What would change if you genuinely reversed the direction?

What does the YOU INC. version of you look like in five years? Write one sentence—not a wish, but a direction.

YOUR ECOSYSTEM

Think of three professional relationships that have genuinely shaped your career. What made them powerful—and are you investing in relationships of similar depth today?

When did you last give something of genuine value to your network without expecting anything in return? What did it produce?

YOUR INFRASTRUCTURE

What systems—not intentions—do you currently have in place for your own development? Be specific. If the answer is none, what is the smallest system you could start this week?

When did you last conduct a Me Inc. Review—an honest stocktake of what developed, what stalled, and what needs to change? If never, set a date now.

A Note Before You Continue

The chapters ahead—Parts 3 through 5—move from understanding the world to navigating it. They deal with uncertainty, identity, experience, and the continuous work of reinvention. The answers you have written here will make those chapters more useful. Not because you will find the answers in the pages that follow, but because you will be reading them as someone who has already asked the right questions of themselves. Your time starts now.

PART 3
Navigating Uncertainty

CHAPTER 7

Black Swans, Grey Rhinos and Silver Linings

There is a conversation I have returned to many times in my mind, though it happened almost casually, at the end of a dinner that had covered a great deal of other ground first.

The man sitting across from me had built a career that looked, from the outside, like a model of deliberate construction. The right institutions, the right roles, the right progression at the right intervals. I said as much. He smiled and shook his head.

> *"It looks very planned from the outside," he said. "But if I am truthful, half of it happened because something unexpected forced me to change direction."*
>
> *He paused, turning his glass slowly on the table.*
>
> *"And the other half happened because I noticed an opportunity that nobody else seemed to see."*
>
> *I found that a remarkably honest thing for a successful person to say. Most people, looking back at careers that worked out well, tend to narrate them as more intentional than they actually were. We smooth the rough edges, connect the dots in hindsight, and present the whole thing as though we knew what we were doing at each turn.*

> *He was not doing that. He was describing the reality that almost every professional, if they are honest with themselves, will recognise.*

Careers are shaped by events we anticipate, events we never see coming, and opportunities that appear quietly in the middle of disruption. The question is not whether any of these will arrive. They will. The question is whether we are prepared to navigate them when they do.

Three ideas have helped me think about this more clearly over the years—the Black Swan, the Grey Rhino, and the Silver Lining.

When the Unexpected Appears

The term Black Swan was popularised to describe events that are rare, unexpected, and deeply disruptive. They arrive without warning and reshape the landscape in ways that almost nobody anticipated. For centuries, Europeans believed all swans were white because that was the only kind they had ever seen. The discovery of black swans in Australia overturned that assumption entirely—and the image became a metaphor for events that challenge what we believe to be certain.

In careers and professional life, Black Swans tend to arrive as sudden shocks. A company restructures overnight. An industry pivots in a direction nobody predicted. A health crisis forces everything to a halt. A technology emerges and quietly makes a generation of skills redundant.

> *Vikram described his own Black Swan to me during one of our conversations, some months after he had begun attending those entrepreneur sessions. His company, for all its historical strength, had been caught badly off-balance by a competitor that had not existed five years earlier.*

> *"We saw it coming," he said, "but we did not believe it. There is a difference."*
>
> *"What do you mean?" I asked.*
>
> *"We talked about the threat in meetings. We acknowledged it in strategy documents. But somewhere we assumed it would not really materialise. That the disruption would stop at the edges of our market and leave the core untouched."*
>
> *It did not. And when the shock arrived, it arrived fast.*

The strange thing about Black Swans, I have observed, is that they are rarely as invisible as they appear in hindsight. More often, the signals were there. What was missing was the willingness to act on them before circumstances made action unavoidable.

Arjun once reflected on the restructuring that had finally pushed him to leave his corporate role. "It was not a surprise," he told me. "I had been watching the organisation shrink its ambitions for two years. The Black Swan was really a very slow bird." I laughed. But the point was astute. We often label events as unexpected when what we really mean is that we preferred not to look too directly at what was coming.

"The art of leaving is the art of living. It is not about being hasty. It is about recognising when a chapter has genuinely ended and having the courage to close it before circumstances close it for you. When you leave on your own terms, you are in a fundamentally different position from when you are left behind by events you chose not to see."

The Threats We See but Ignore

If Black Swans represent the unexpected, Grey Rhinos represent something almost more unsettling. A Grey Rhino is a large, obvious threat that has been charging toward you for a considerable time. It is visible. It has been discussed. In many cases, it has been documented in reports and raised in meetings and acknowledged by everyone in the room. And yet it is ignored—until the moment it is impossible to ignore any longer.

The metaphor is deliberately physical. A rhino is not subtle. It is enormous, it makes a great deal of noise as it moves, and it announces its direction well in advance. The problem is not that people cannot see it. The problem is that they find reasons not to act on what they see.

In organisations, Grey Rhinos appear as declining markets that leaders convince themselves will recover, as technologies that threaten the core business but are dismissed as niche, as cultural problems that everyone privately acknowledges but nobody officially addresses.

In individual careers, they are equally familiar. The professional who knows, deep down, that their skills are becoming less relevant but finds reasons to postpone learning something new. The one who can see that their industry is contracting but waits for a definitive sign before beginning to look elsewhere. The one who senses that their current environment has stopped offering growth but stays because leaving feels complicated.

I recognise this pattern partly because I have felt it myself. There have been moments in my career when I have known something needed to change and chosen the comfort of the present over the uncertainty of the next step. The Grey Rhino was in full view. I simply found the ground immediately underfoot more familiar than whatever lay behind it.

> *Meera had lived this too, though her version was more complex. She told me that in the two years before she eventually took her break, she had known that something was unsustainable. The signals were clear—exhaustion that did not lift, a growing sense of going through motions, a feeling that the work was no longer connecting to anything she genuinely valued.*
>
> *"But I kept telling myself it would pass," she said. "That next quarter would be different. That I just needed one good project to remind me why I was there."*
>
> *"And did it come?"*
>
> *"No," she said simply. "Because the problem was not the project. The problem was that I had stayed past the point where the role still fit."*
>
> *The Grey Rhino had been visible for two years. It took another year before she was ready to stop pretending otherwise.*

The lesson is not that we should panic at every warning sign. It is that awareness and early action are almost always less costly than waiting until circumstances force the issue. The organisation that addresses a Grey Rhino while it is still some distance away has options. The one that waits until it is at the door does not.

Finding the Silver Linings

Crises and disruptions rarely feel positive while they are happening. It would be facile to suggest otherwise. But history—personal history as much as the broader kind—is full of examples where difficult circumstances have produced opportunities that would never have appeared in calmer times. Not despite the disruption but because of it.

This is the Silver Lining. And I want to be precise about what I mean by it because the phrase is sometimes used to paper over genuine difficulty with forced optimism. A Silver Lining is not the denial of pain. It is the recognition that within disruption, once the dust begins to settle, there are often possibilities that were simply not visible before. New directions that the previous path had obscured. Capabilities discovered under pressure that would never have been tested in comfort. Relationships formed in adversity that turn out to be among the most durable.

Arjun found his Silver Lining slowly and reluctantly. Eighteen months into his consulting venture, the thing he had not expected was the quality of the conversations he was now having. Without the institutional identity of a large company behind him, he was meeting people differently. There was no corporate armour to retreat behind. Every conversation was, in some sense, personal. "I have learned more about how I actually think in the last eighteen months than in the previous 12 years," he told me. "Because of the difficulty?" I asked. "Because of the exposure," he said. "The difficulty was the vehicle. What it delivered was clarity."

Meera's Silver Lining was different, and in some ways more quietly profound. The four years away from formal employment had been demanding in ways that a corporate career never quite prepares you for. But they had also given her something she had not anticipated: a quality of self-knowledge that she was only now beginning to articulate. "I know what I am made of now," she said during one of our conversations. "I did not know that before. I thought I did. But I had never actually been tested." She said it without drama, as a simple statement of fact. And it was one of the most confident things I had heard from her, which was saying something.

Three Forces at Work

Black Swans, Grey Rhinos and Silver Linings represent three distinct forces that shape careers and lives. And they are worth holding together, because each one, in isolation, tells an incomplete story.

The Black Swan, considered alone, produces fatalism. If truly unexpected events will occur regardless of what we do, why bother preparing at all? The Grey Rhino, considered alone, produces anxiety. If obvious threats are everywhere and we are all ignoring them, how does one know where to look? The Silver Lining, considered alone, produces something almost worse—a breezy optimism that refuses to take difficulty seriously.

But together, they produce something useful. A more honest account of how professional life unfolds, and a more grounded basis for navigating it. Unexpected things will happen. Some threats are visible if we are willing to look. And within disruption, if we stay curious and alert, opportunities do appear. This is not a guarantee of smooth passage. It is simply an accurate map of the terrain.

A Conversation About Uncertainty

Aarav raised the question that many people carry but fewer ask out loud, during a session I was running for a group of final-year students. It was asked with genuine seriousness. He was not being provocative. He was, for once, genuinely uncertain about something—which, given how much he usually radiated confidence, I found rather encouraging.

> *"How do you plan a career when so many things are unpredictable?" he asked.*
>
> *I thought about it for a moment before answering. "Tell me," I said, "how do you think well-run organisations plan in environments they cannot fully predict?"*
>
> *He considered this. "I suppose they try to be ready for different scenarios."*

> *"More than that," I said. "They focus less on predicting the future and more on building the capacity to respond to it, whatever it brings. They invest in resilience, adaptability, and the kind of internal strength that travels across different circumstances."*
>
> *He nodded slowly. "So the goal is not to predict correctly," he said. "The goal is to be the kind of person who can handle being wrong."*
>
> *I thought that was rather well put. Better, if I am honest, than I had put it myself.*
>
> *Zara, who was sitting nearby, added quietly, "That is actually more reassuring than a plan."*
>
> *She was right. A plan assumes a particular future. Resilience works in any of them.*

Resilience as a Strategic Asset

Resilience is often described as the ability to recover from setbacks. That is accurate, as far as it goes. But I think of it more broadly than that. Resilience is the capacity to remain functional, curious, and forward-looking even when circumstances change in ways you did not choose and would not have wished for.

Organisations cultivate it by diversifying their capabilities, maintaining financial stability, and building teams that can adjust to new conditions without losing their core purpose. Individuals can do something similar. Learning continuously strengthens adaptability—not because any particular skill will necessarily prove relevant, but because the habit of learning itself keeps the mind flexible. Maintaining genuine relationships provides perspective and support during difficult periods in ways that are very hard to manufacture in a crisis. Building financial stability, however modest, reduces the kind of vulnerability that forces bad decisions under pressure.

None of these prevent uncertainty. But they change its texture considerably. The professionals who have invested in their own resilience do not face disruption from a standing start. They face it with resources—internal and external—that make a genuine difference to what comes next.

Paying Attention to Signals

One thing I have noticed in professionals who navigate uncertainty well is that they tend to be good listeners—not just in conversation, but in the broader sense. They pay attention to what is changing around them before it becomes obvious.

> *Naren described this during one of our conversations. He had spent decades in leadership, and I asked him what habit he thought had served him best across the long arc of his career.*
>
> *"Paying attention to things at the edges," he said.*
>
> *"What do you mean by edges?" I asked.*
>
> *"The conversations people have casually before they become the agenda. The concerns that are raised once and then dropped. The new ideas that are dismissed quickly in a meeting—those especially, because usually the dismissal is a sign that someone is unsettled, not that the idea has no merit."*
>
> *He paused, then added, "The future usually announces itself quietly, well before it arrives loudly. The people who are listening at the right volume hear it earlier."*

That habit—of listening widely, of staying genuinely curious about what is shifting at the periphery—is one of the most underrated capabilities in professional life. It is not strategic planning. It is something more like attentiveness. And in a world that changes quickly and irregularly, attentiveness is a form of competitive advantage.

Preparing for the Unknown

Despite everything—the planning, resilience, and the attention to signals—uncertainty will always remain part of life. Black Swans will arrive uninvited. Grey Rhinos will occasionally be ignored until they are very close indeed. And Silver Linings will appear in places we did not think to look, at moments we would not have chosen.

What we can control is our readiness to respond. The inner infrastructure, as the previous chapter described—the learning habits, the resilience built from experience, the relationships maintained through genuine investment—does not eliminate the unpredictable. But it changes what we are capable of when the unpredictable arrives.

The man at that dinner said something as we were leaving. "The strange thing about uncertainty," he said, putting on his jacket, "is that it often opens doors you did not even know existed." He was not suggesting that disruption should be welcomed uncritically. He knew, as anyone who has lived through difficult professional periods knows, that the experience is rarely pleasant while it is happening.

But there was something in the way he said it that was neither resigned nor falsely cheerful. It was the observation of someone who had lived through enough uncertainty to have made a kind of peace with it—not by pretending it was comfortable, but by discovering, repeatedly, that it was navigable. That discovery, I have come to believe, is one of the most valuable things a professional life can offer. You do not find it in the smooth passages. You find it in the difficult ones.

KEY TAKEAWAYS

- Black Swans rarely arrive without warning—the signals are usually there. What is missing is the willingness to act on them before circumstances force the issue.
- Grey Rhinos are the threats we see clearly but choose not to confront. Early action is almost always less costly than waiting until they are impossible to ignore.
- Silver Linings are not forced optimism. They are the genuine possibilities that disruption reveals—new directions, discovered capabilities, and relationships formed under pressure that turn out to be the most durable.
- Resilience is a strategic asset, built deliberately through learning habits, maintained relationships, and the accumulated evidence that you have navigated difficulty before and can do so again.

The three forces described in this chapter will all appear in your professional life. They already have. The question is not whether they will come again. It is whether you will meet them with the infrastructure and orientation to turn each one into something useful.

REFLECT ON THIS

1. Think of a Black Swan in your own career—something that reshaped your path without warning. Looking back, were there signals you chose not to see? What would you do differently?

2. What is the Grey Rhino currently visible in your career or industry that you have been finding reasons to ignore? What would it cost to address it now versus in two years?

3. Where has disruption—a setback, a forced change, an unexpected ending—ultimately opened a door you would not otherwise have found? What did that teach you?

CHAPTER 8

The Gift of the Present

Shoma has a particular way of ending certain conversations. She does not raise her voice. She does not make a lengthy argument. She simply looks at me with an expression that manages to be simultaneously affectionate and devastating, and says four words.

"So, when do you start?"

I have been on the receiving end of this question more times than I care to count. It has arrived after I have spent an evening explaining, with great thoroughness, why a particular idea needs more thought. Why the timing is not quite right. Why another few weeks of reflection would be prudent before committing to anything. She is not unsympathetic to any of this. She listens to every word. And then she asks her question.

Over the years I have come to understand that it is not really a question at all. It is a gentle, firm, and entirely accurate observation that at some point thinking becomes a way of not doing—and that the present moment, imperfect as it always feels, is where everything that actually matters eventually has to begin.

The Illusion of Perfect Timing

It is entirely natural to want conditions to be favourable before acting. We prefer clarity to ambiguity and like to feel prepared. We hope that circumstances will align in ways that reduce the risk and sharpen the odds before we commit to anything significant. But waiting for perfect conditions has a way of quietly becoming a habit—and habits tend to persist long past the point where they are serving any useful purpose.

Aarav came to me with exactly this problem, about six months after I had first met him in that classroom. He had, by this point, a newsletter with a modest but growing readership, a small freelance project that was going reasonably well, and an idea for something larger that he had been turning over in his mind for several months.

"I want to build something properly," he said. "Not just the newsletter. A proper platform. Courses, maybe. A community."

"That sounds worth doing," I said.

"I think so too." He paused. "I just want to get a few more things in place first."

"What things?"

He listed them. More subscribers. More clarity on the audience. A better understanding of the technology involved. Perhaps one more big freelance project to build credibility.

I let him finish.

"Aarav," I said, "what you have just described is not preparation. It is postponement wearing preparation's clothes."

He looked slightly stung.

"The clarity you are waiting for," I told him, "will not arrive before you begin. It will arrive because you begin.

> *Those are very different propositions, and only one of them leads anywhere."*
>
> *He was quiet for a moment. Then he said, "So you are telling me to jump without looking."*
>
> *"I am telling you to look while jumping," I said. "Which is what most worthwhile things in life actually require."*

Action Creates Clarity

One of the most underestimated qualities of action is the clarity it generates. When we remain in the realm of ideas, possibilities tend to appear both enormous and strangely shapeless. There are too many variables to weigh, too many potential outcomes to predict, too many ways the thing could go wrong to feel fully comfortable proceeding.

The moment we take a step—however modest—the situation changes character entirely. We receive feedback. We discover what we did not know we did not know. We find that certain fears were reasonable and others were entirely imaginary. We learn which parts of our plan were well-designed and which were optimistic fiction. Action transforms uncertainty into information. And information, however uncomfortable, is almost always more useful than the clean but inert state of waiting.

> *Zara understood this instinctively, which was one of the things I found most impressive about her. She had not waited to feel ready before building her content practice. She had built it, and allowed the practice itself to teach her what she needed to know.*

> *"The first few months were genuinely terrible," she told me cheerfully. "The content was inconsistent. The audience was tiny. I had no idea what I was doing."*
>
> *"And now?"*
>
> *"Now I have a slightly better idea of what I am doing," she said. "Which is more than I would have if I had spent those six months planning."*
>
> *She said it simply, without particular pride—as a plain statement of how things worked. And she was right. The learning she had accumulated through doing could not have been replicated through any amount of prior thinking.*

"Work as worship—process purity is more important than the morbidity of the desired result. The quality of how you show up each day matters more than anxiously watching for the outcome."

The Courage to Begin

Acting in uncertain conditions requires a particular kind of courage. The courage I am describing is quieter than the dramatic leap. It is the willingness to begin before everything feels comfortable. To take the first step knowing that the second step will only become visible once the first has been taken.

Meera had this quality in abundance, though she had not always recognised it as courage. She had returned to the workforce in a climate that was not especially welcoming of her specific situation—the gap on the CV, the years away, the industry that had changed in her absence. Every reasonable analysis of her circumstances suggested she wait until conditions improved.

She did not wait.

"I decided," she told me, "that conditions were not going to improve on their own. The gap was not going to become less visible with time. The only thing that was going to change the situation was movement."

She had started by reaching out to her network—not with a polished pitch, but with a simple, honest message. That she was returning, that she was keen to reconnect, and that she was interested in what people were working on. No elaborate strategy. Just a first step.

From those conversations, one thing had led to another. A coffee had become a consulting conversation. A consulting conversation had become a small project. A small project had become a proper engagement.

"Was it exactly what you had planned?" I asked.

She laughed. "It was nothing like what I had planned. It was better."

That is something I have noticed repeatedly about meaningful professional progress. The path that unfolds when you begin is almost never the one you imagined before you started. It is shaped by what you find along the way—and you find those things only by moving.

The Power of Initiative

There is a version of professional life in which one waits to be asked—for permission, for instruction, for someone in authority to identify that a contribution is needed and to formally request it. And there is another version, considerably more interesting, in which one sees where something useful can be done and simply does it.

Initiative, in my experience, is one of the most powerful signals a professional can send—not because it is strategically calculated to impress, but because it reflects a genuine orientation toward contribution rather than compliance.

> *Naren said something about this during one of our conversations that I thought captured it precisely. We were talking about the leaders he had most valued over his career—not the ones with the most impressive credentials, but the ones who had created genuine movement in organisations.*
>
> *"They did not wait to be pointed at a problem," he said. "They arrived having already thought about it. Sometimes having already begun to solve it."*
>
> *"Was that not occasionally overstepping?" I asked.*
>
> *"Sometimes," he said. "And when it was, the good ones acknowledged it and adjusted. But the energy behind it was always right. They cared enough to act without being asked." He paused. "That is very rare. And it is noticed."*

Initiative does not require seniority or permission. It requires only attentiveness—seeing where something useful can be done—and the willingness to do it without waiting for someone else to make it official.

Experiments, Not Commitments

One reason people hesitate to act is the fear that action represents a permanent commitment. That taking a step means being bound to the direction it points in, regardless of what is discovered along the way. This is, in my experience, a significant overestimation of what any single action commits you to.

The YOU INC. mindset is not the mindset of the grand, irreversible gesture. It is the mindset of the organisation in permanent beta: continuously experimenting, learning from what each experiment produces, and using that learning to inform the next iteration.

> *Arjun had learned this, though the learning had not been entirely comfortable. When he left his corporate role, he had imagined the transition as a definitive crossing—from one clearly defined identity to another. What he had found instead was something more iterative. His consulting firm had evolved considerably from the version he had launched 18 months earlier. Two of his initial service offerings had been quietly retired. One that he had not originally planned had become the core of the business.*
>
> *"I thought leaving was the decision," he told me. "What I discovered is that leaving was just the first decision. There have been dozens since."*
>
> *"And that bothers you?"*
>
> *"It used to," he said. "Now I think it is just how it works. You do not plan your way to clarity. You experiment your way there."*

An experiment is a different psychological proposition from a commitment. It carries less weight, allows for adjustment, and positions whatever happens—success or setback—as information rather than verdict. And information, unlike verdict, can be used.

The Present as the Only Available Starting Point

There is a temptation—particularly among people who think carefully about things—to treat the present as somehow insufficient. As a waiting room for the future, rather than the place where the future is actually being made.

I have felt this myself. The present is always imperfect. There is always something that is not yet in place, some capability that is not yet developed, some condition that would improve if given more time to mature. This is simply true. It is also, if allowed to become the primary way of experiencing the present, a very effective way of not doing anything at all.

> *I mentioned this to Shoma one evening, during one of those conversations that begin about something else and gradually find their way to something more important.*
>
> *"You always say that," she observed.*
>
> *"Because it is always true," I said.*
>
> *"Yes," she said. "But the interesting question is why people find it so difficult to actually do."*
>
> *I thought about this.*

> *"Because the present is where the risk lives," I said eventually. "The future is imaginary. You can arrange it however you like. The present is real. If you act in it and the thing does not work, you know."*
>
> *She considered this. "So, the present feels more dangerous than the future."*
>
> *"Precisely. Even though it is the only place where anything can actually happen."*
>
> *She returned to her book. "So, when do you start?" she said, without looking up.*

The Quiet Gift

When we reflect on the moments that turned out to matter most in our professional lives, there is a tendency to give them, in hindsight, a quality of drama they did not possess at the time. Most of those moments began as ordinary days. Unremarkable mornings on which someone decided to send the message, start the project, make the call, take the first step toward something they had been thinking about for too long.

The present is not glamorous. It does not promise outcomes. It offers only the possibility of motion—and motion, in an uncertain world, is itself a form of advantage.

Aarav sent me a message some weeks after our conversation about his platform idea. He had started. Not the full version, not the perfectly designed thing he had been imagining—just a first version, rough-edged and imperfect, put into the world to see what it would attract. "It is not ready," he wrote. "But I remembered what you said about the clarity arriving because you begin, not before." He was right to remember it. Because what came back to him from that imperfect first version—the responses, the interest, the unexpected directions it opened—was worth more than any amount of further planning could have produced.

The present, he was discovering, was not the waiting room. It was the thing itself.

KEY TAKEAWAYS

- Clarity does not precede action. It follows from it. The professional who waits to feel fully ready is waiting for something that rarely arrives on schedule.
- Initiative—seeing where something useful can be done and doing it without waiting to be asked—is one of the most powerful signals a professional can send.
- Think of early actions as experiments, not commitments. Experiments generate information. Information is more useful than any plan built in the absence of it.
- The present is the only available starting point. Treating it as a waiting room is not caution. It is a very effective way of not doing anything at all.

The chapters ahead deal with identity, reputation, experience, and reinvention—all of which require the same thing that this chapter has been arguing for. Not a perfect plan, but a first step. Not ideal conditions, but the willingness to begin in the conditions that actually exist.

REFLECT ON THIS

1. What is something you have been thinking about starting—a project, a conversation, a change—that you have been waiting on until conditions feel right? What would it look like to start an imperfect version of it this week?

2. Think of a time when action produced clarity you could not have reached through planning alone. What did that teach you about the relationship between movement and understanding?

3. Where in your professional life are you currently waiting to be asked rather than simply beginning? What is the cost of that waiting?

PART 4
Building Your Identity

CHAPTER 9

Vision and Execution

Strategy fascinates people. Executives attend conferences to discuss it. Consultants design elaborate frameworks to explain it. Business schools devote entire courses to analysing it. Vision statements are crafted with great care, presentations are built around them, and impressive diagrams are drawn on whiteboards that are photographed and then never looked at again.

Yet after many years of observing organisations and the people who lead them, I have concluded that sounds almost too simple to be worth stating. Strategy matters only when it leads to action. A beautifully articulated vision that never reaches the ground remains, at best, an intellectual exercise. At worst, it becomes a substitute for the harder and less glamorous work of actually doing something.

> *I was reminded of this during a conversation with Vikram, not long after he had begun his period of deliberate renewal. He had just come from a two-day strategy offsite at his organisation—the kind of event that involves a great deal of structured thinking, large sheets of paper covered in coloured markers, and a catered lunch that everyone agrees was rather good. He did not look energised.*
>
> *"How was it?" I asked.*

> *He thought for a moment. "Interesting," he said, in the tone people use when they mean the opposite.*
>
> *"What happened?"*
>
> *"We spent two days deciding what we want to become," he said. "Very ambitious. Very well-presented. On the drive back, I tried to remember whether anyone had said a single specific thing about what we would actually do differently on Monday morning."*
>
> *He paused. "I could not think of one."*

The Distance between Intention and Reality

The gap between strategy and execution is one of the most persistent problems in organisational life. It is also, in my observation, one of the most underestimated. Most organisations do not fail because they lack ideas. They fail because they cannot close the distance between the idea and its implementation. The plan is sophisticated. The presentation is polished. The room is aligned. And then Monday morning arrives, and everyone returns to doing more or less what they were doing before.

This is not a failure of intelligence. It is a failure of the bridge between thinking and acting. Individuals experience precisely the same problem. The gap between knowing what you should do and actually doing it is where most professional development quietly goes to die. The YOU INC. framework is, in its practical dimension, largely about closing that gap. The purpose, goals, systems, the annual review—none of these are interesting as ideas. They are interesting only when they produce different behaviour. Which is to say, only when they are executed.

For a long time, organisations believed that analysing what had worked in the past was sufficient to navigate the future. Today the pace of change makes that assumption increasingly fragile.

Technologies emerge from unexpected directions. Consumer behaviour shifts before organisations can track it. This is why strategic thinking today requires imagination as much as analysis—not the imagination of idle fantasy, but the disciplined imagination of someone who asks: given what I can see, and given what I cannot yet see, what is the wisest way to prepare?

The Seduction of the Perfect Plan

One of the most common failures in strategic thinking is the pursuit of certainty before commitment. I have seen this pattern many times. A leader or a team spends months—sometimes years—trying to anticipate every possible outcome before taking a first step. The analysis becomes increasingly sophisticated. The caveats accumulate. The scenarios multiply. And somewhere in the middle of all that thoroughness, the moment passes.

> *Arjun described a version of this from his corporate years. There was a digital initiative he had championed—something that, in retrospect, would have positioned his organisation considerably better for the changes that followed. But the proposal kept getting sent back for further analysis. More data was needed. The business case required refinement. The timing needed to be better understood.*
>
> *"It took eighteen months to approve," he told me. "By which time two competitors had already launched something similar and were twelve months into learning from it."*
>
> *"What was the organisation afraid of?" I asked.*

> *"Getting it wrong," he said simply. "Which is funny, because by waiting they guaranteed getting it wrong. They just got it wrong more expensively and more slowly."*

Strategy as a Series of Experiments

One of the ideas that has most influenced my thinking over the years is the notion that strategy is not a single decision but a series of experiments. Organisations operate in environments that are too complex and too fast-moving to be fully understood in advance. Rigid, comprehensive planning—the kind that assumes a fixed future and builds every decision around that assumption—is not only unhelpful but genuinely dangerous. It creates false confidence and makes organisations slow to respond when reality diverges from the plan, which it inevitably does.

> **"Alternative simulation of realities is important. If one already knows the answer, the question is probably wrong. Hold multiple possible futures simultaneously and prepare for several things that might happen, rather than planning brilliantly for one that may not."**

> *The first time Aarav heard me say that he laughed. "Sir, that is a very complicated way of saying 'have a backup plan,'" he said.*

"In essence, yes," I told him, smiling. "But the idea goes slightly further. A backup plan assumes a primary plan that will probably work, with a secondary option in reserve. What I am describing is a more fundamental orientation—one in which you hold multiple possible futures simultaneously and think carefully about what each of them would require of you."

He considered this. "So, it is less about predicting what will happen and more about preparing for several things that might."

"Precisely. The organisation—or the individual—that has genuinely imagined how they would respond to three different futures is considerably more resilient than the one that has planned brilliantly for one."

Zara had internalised something like this instinctively in how she built her professional life. She had not staked everything on a single version of her future. The content practice, the management degree, the consulting conversations she was beginning to have—these were not a scattered collection of activities. They were, she had once described to me, deliberate bets on different possible versions of where things might go.

"If one path closes," she said, "I have others I have already been developing."

"That is not hedging," I told her. "That is intelligence."

The Discipline of Execution

While vision concerns the future, execution belongs firmly to the present. Execution is the discipline of turning intention into action. It requires focus, consistency, and a willingness to engage with the unglamorous details that large ideas tend to obscure. It does not attract the same intellectual admiration as strategy—there are no conferences dedicated to the art of following through, no frameworks named after execution theorists. But without it, strategy is nothing more than an expensive conversation.

The most effective leaders I have worked with and observed over the years share a quality that is easy to overlook precisely because it is not dramatic. They finish things. Not everything—no one finishes everything. But the things they commit to, they complete. They follow through on the initiatives they launch and keep the promises they make. And this consistency, sustained over years, produces a level of institutional trust that no strategy document can manufacture.

> *Naren embodied this. When I asked him once what quality he looked for most in the leaders he developed during his long career, I expected him to say vision, or intelligence, or the ability to inspire.*
>
> *He said: "Finish rate."*
>
> *I was not sure I had heard correctly. "Finish rate?"*
>
> *"The ratio of things started to things completed," he said. "It is more revealing than almost anything else. A person with a high finish rate, even if they are not the most visionary thinker in the room, will outperform a brilliant strategist who cannot close things off. Every time."*
>
> *He was quiet for a moment. "The graveyard of corporate life is full of people who had excellent ideas. Far fewer people have the discipline to see them through."*

The Psychology of Progress

Execution also requires a particular inner discipline—one that is harder to maintain than people generally expect. Large strategic visions can overwhelm. When the goal feels distant and the path long, motivation has a way of quietly eroding. The ambitious target that seemed energising in January becomes dispiriting by March if there is no visible movement in the interim.

This is why the most effective leaders break ambitious visions into sequences of manageable steps. Not because the ambition is scaled back, but because progress needs to be felt as well as measured. The team that can see that it is moving—that last week they were here and this week they are there—maintains an energy that abstract goal setting cannot sustain.

I borrow a phrase from sport to describe this. In cricket, tennis, or golf—any game in which performance is measured over a long series of individual actions—the best practitioners share a common discipline. They do not allow themselves to become distracted by the final score, the championship, or the career landmark. They concentrate on the next ball, the next point, the next hole. The long-term goal provides direction. But the next shot is where the game is realistically played. Strategic execution works in the same way.

Aarav had applied this—perhaps without quite realising it—in the weeks after we had spoken about his platform idea. Rather than continuing to plan the full version, he had committed to one specific action: launching a first, imperfect iteration and getting feedback from 50 people within 30 days. That was the next shot. He messaged me when he had done it. "It is not ready," he wrote. "But it is out. And I already know three things I would do differently, which I could not have known from the inside." That is what the next shot produces: information.

Aligning Vision and Action

The most effective leaders I have observed possess an unusual quality. They can hold the long view and the immediate detail simultaneously—moving fluently between the two without losing either. They can speak about where the organisation is heading in terms that are genuinely inspiring and then sit down and work through the specific decisions that need to be made this week to move in that direction. The two modes of thinking reinforce each other rather than competing.

Vision without execution is illusion. But execution without vision is equally limiting—it produces activity without direction, motion without meaning. People work hard, things get done, and yet somehow the organisation does not arrive anywhere in particular.

> *Meera had done this instinctively during her re-entry. She had not planned each step in sequence. She had held a clear sense of what kind of work she wanted to be doing and what kind of professional she wanted to be—and then made each decision considering that orientation. The coffee conversations, small projects, and the advisory conversations—none of these were steps in a plan. They were steps toward a direction.*
>
> *"I did not know exactly where I was going," she told me once. "But I always knew roughly which way I was facing. That turned out to be enough."*

The Conversation That Never Ends

Toward the end of one of our longer conversations, Aarav asked me the question I had been expecting him to ask for some time. "Sir, is vision or execution more important?" I told him, as I always tell people who ask this question, that it is probably the wrong question. Vision and execution are not competing priorities. They are complementary capabilities—each incomplete without the other. Vision provides direction. Execution provides momentum.

"So how do you maintain that connection?" he asked.

"By checking in with both, regularly," I said. "Every so often, stop and ask whether what you are doing today is actually moving you toward where you said you wanted to go. And every so often, ask whether where you said you wanted to go is still actually where you want to go. Both questions matter. Neither one, alone, is sufficient."

He nodded slowly. "That sounds like a lot of reflection," he said.

"It is," I agreed. "Which is why most people do not do it."

He smiled at that. And then he picked up his pen.

KEY TAKEAWAYS

- Strategy without execution is intellectual decoration. The gap between knowing what to do and actually doing it is where most professional development goes to die.
- Holding multiple possible futures simultaneously—and preparing for several—is more resilient than planning brilliantly for one. Alternative simulation is not pessimism. It is intelligence.
- Finish rate is one of the most revealing measures of professional quality. Completing what you commit to, consistently and without drama, builds a kind of trust that no amount of vision can substitute for.
- Vision and execution are not competing priorities. They are complementary capabilities. Direction without movement stalls. Movement without direction wanders. Both are required.

Strategy, at its most useful, is not a document or a presentation. It is a habit of mind—the ongoing discipline of asking whether what you are doing today is actually connected to where you are trying to go. Combined with the execution discipline of following through, it becomes something genuinely powerful: a professional life that is designed, not merely accumulated.

REFLECT ON THIS

1. What is the gap between your stated direction and your daily behaviour? If someone observed you for a week without knowing your stated goals, what would they conclude those goals were?

2. Think of something significant you started in the past two years but did not finish. What got in the way—and what does your finish rate say about where your focus lies?

3. Where are you currently holding multiple possible futures for your career? And where are you planning rigidly for one version of the future as though it is guaranteed?

CHAPTER 10

Personal Brand and Reputation

There is an old colleague of mine—a man I worked alongside for nearly a decade in the early years of my corporate life—who said something at a farewell dinner that I have never quite been able to put down.

We were there for a mutual friend who was moving on after a long and distinguished stint at our organisation. The evening was warm, the speeches were generous, the food was adequate, and at some point, my colleague leaned across the table and said, almost to himself, "You know what the most durable thing about him is? Not any campaign he ran. Not any award he won. It is the way people feel when they talk about him."

I looked around the room as he said it. There were perhaps 60 people there, drawn from different decades of our friend's career, from different industries and cities. Most of them had not seen each other in years. Yet they were gathered, on a weeknight, to mark his leaving. That, I realised, was the reputation in the room. Not the plaques on the wall nor the titles on the programme. The sixty people who had made the effort.

What Reputation Actually Is

There was a time when reputation travelled at a measured pace. It moved through institutions, through word of mouth, and through the slow accumulation of small observations over years. A person built it quietly and the world assessed it patiently. That world no longer exists.

Today reputation moves at the speed of a forwarded message. A poorly handled moment in a video call can ripple outward in ways that would have seemed improbable a decade ago. Equally, a single thoughtful act—a well-chosen response in a difficult situation, a piece of work that demonstrates genuine quality—can travel across networks we did not even know we belonged to.

> *Aarav asked me about this directly, during one of our conversations after a session. He had that combination of earnestness and mild anxiety that tends to accompany his better questions.*
>
> *"Sir, I keep reading that I need to build a personal brand. Should I be more active on LinkedIn? Post more content?"*
>
> *"That depends," I told him. "Are you putting something out there worth discovering? Or are you just making noise?"*
>
> *He thought about this.*
>
> *"The brand," I continued, "is not what you post. It is what people say about you when you are not in the room."*
>
> *He was quiet for a moment. Then: "So the posting is not the brand."*
>
> *"The posting, at best, is evidence of the brand. At worst, it is a distraction from building it. The question worth asking is not how visible you are, but whether there is substance behind the visibility."*

In a world saturated with self-promotion, genuine reputation has become rarer and more precious than ever. Which means the individual who actually builds it—quietly, consistently, through the quality of their work and the honesty of their conduct—has a more significant advantage than at any previous moment in professional history.

The Myth of Talent

We live in a culture that has developed a near-religious attachment to the idea of talent. Young people are told, from very early in their education, that the key to success is discovering their unique gift and pursuing it with passion. There is some truth in this. But it conceals a more inconvenient reality. Talent opens a door. It does not guarantee what lies on the other side.

I have known brilliant people who never quite fulfilled the promise their early careers suggested. I have also known individuals of perfectly ordinary natural ability who built reputations of extraordinary durability. The difference, in almost every case, was not talent. It was something considerably less glamorous.

> **"Success has an inbuilt learning disability. The habits, assumptions, and approaches that produced yesterday's wins can quietly prevent us from seeing what today's situation actually requires."**

> *Vikram understood this, though he had understood it as an abstraction for many years before he felt it as a reality. When I met him again some months into his renewal—the entrepreneur sessions, the deliberate discomfort of being the oldest person in the room—he reflected on what he had been slowly realising about his own trajectory.*

> *"I built my reputation on a run of good years," he said. "Strong results, the right projects, the right organisation behind me. But I think at some point I started assuming the reputation would sustain itself. That it was—I don't know—permanent."*
>
> *"And is it?"*
>
> *"No," he said simply. "It is only permanent if you keep earning it." He paused. "That sounds obvious when you say it out loud."*
>
> *"Most important things do," I said.*

The professional who delivers reliably, who meets their commitments without drama, who shows up prepared and treats every assignment seriously regardless of its size, is the professional who earns lasting trust. And trust, once earned, becomes a quiet but formidable form of competitive advantage—the kind that no amount of self-promotion can replicate or replace.

Preparation as Character

Behind every polished performance lies a great deal of invisible work. I learnt this relatively early, though not through any formal instruction. I learnt it by watching the people I most admired and noticing what they had in common. They were almost always the most prepared people in any room. Not the most confident. Not the loudest. Not necessarily the most naturally gifted. The most prepared.

> *Shoma once watched me prepare for a particularly important presentation many years ago. I had been at it for most of the evening, rearranging arguments, reconsidering examples, pacing around the living room testing sentences out loud.*
>
> *"You are doing it again," she said, not unkindly.*
>
> *"Doing what?" I asked.*
>
> *"Preparing as though everything depends on it."*
>
> *She smiled. "Go to bed, Bhaskar. You are ready."*
>
> *I did not always agree with her timeline. But she was right about the underlying point. At some stage, preparation gives way to presence. And presence, on the day, is what people actually remember.*

Preparation communicates something important to everyone observing it. It says: I take this seriously. I respect your time. I have done the thinking before asking you to do the listening. In high-stakes moments, this pays dividends that are difficult to quantify but impossible to miss. The person who has genuinely prepared moves through it with a quality of calm that others feel without quite being able to name.

The Digital Dimension

The connected world has introduced a layer of complexity to reputation that previous generations never had to navigate. Professional identity no longer resides solely within the four walls of a workplace. It extends into digital spaces that carry our ideas, our opinions, our associations, and occasionally our more unguarded moments to audiences that stretch far beyond our immediate circles.

> *Zara had thought about this more carefully than most people her age, which I found both impressive and unsurprising. She had been building her content practice for long enough to have moved past the initial instinct to post frequently and hope for the best.*
>
> *"In the beginning," she told me, "I posted a lot. Anything that seemed interesting. I wanted to be visible."*
>
> *"And now?"*
>
> *"Now I only share something if it is genuinely what I think. If it adds something I have not seen elsewhere. If I would be comfortable with anyone—including people who disagree with me—reading it."*
>
> *"That is a much higher bar," I observed.*
>
> *"It is also a much more sustainable one," she said. "I post less. But the quality of the conversations it starts is completely different."*

She had arrived, through instinct and experience, at what I think is the most important principle for managing a professional presence in the digital world. The professionals who do it best are not the most active. They are the most intentional. They share what they genuinely believe. They engage with ideas they actually find interesting. And they remain consistent, in their digital behaviour as in everything else, with the person they are actually trying to become.

The Danger of the Finished Product

One of the most seductive traps in professional life is the feeling of arrival. After years of building skills, establishing credibility, and earning recognition, it is tempting to believe that the hard work is largely done. That one has, in some meaningful sense, made it. That the reputation is now an asset that can be drawn upon rather than an account that requires continuous investment. I have watched this trap close around some genuinely talented people. The moment they stopped evolving, their relevance began—imperceptibly at first, then more rapidly—to erode.

> *Naren had seen this from the other side—the long view of someone who had watched careers unfold over decades. We were talking one afternoon about the leaders he had most admired and those who had, despite considerable early promise, fallen short of what they might have been.*
>
> *"The saddest cases," he said, "were the ones who stopped being curious. Who reached a certain level and decided they had arrived at the answers. They were often brilliant people. But they became—what is the word—impermeable."*
>
> *"Nothing got in," I said.*
>
> *"Nothing got in," he confirmed. "Which meant nothing changed. Which meant that eventually the world moved on without them, and they were left holding a reputation that described someone from a previous decade."*
>
> *"Did you feel that pull yourself?" I asked.*

> *He considered this for a moment. "I felt it at around fifty," he said. "There was a period when I noticed I was mostly confirming things I already believed rather than genuinely questioning them. I caught it, I think, before it became permanent. But it required someone to say something uncomfortable first."*
>
> *"Who said it?"*
>
> *He smiled. "My youngest daughter. She was about twenty-two at the time. She said, 'Papa, you have the same opinion about everything.' She was not being unkind. She was being accurate."*
>
> *He paused. "Daughters," he said, "are underrated as strategic advisors."*

What Recovery Reveals

Professional life, for almost everyone, includes failures. Campaigns that do not land. Initiatives that stall. Roles that end earlier than expected. Decisions that, in retrospect, were clearly wrong. The conventional response to failure is to treat it as something to be minimised, explained away, or quietly forgotten as quickly as possible. I have come to believe this is a mistake.

How a professional handles a setback is, in many ways, more revealing than how they handle success. Success is relatively easy to manage with grace. Failure requires something more substantial: the honesty to acknowledge it, the composure to not be destroyed by it, and the discipline to focus on what comes next rather than on the wound itself.

> *Arjun had learnt this in the most direct possible way. His consulting venture had included several early failures that he had initially found humiliating. A pitch that he lost badly to a competitor he had underestimated. A client engagement that ended because he had overpromised and underdelivered on one dimension. A hire that had not worked out.*
>
> *"In the corporate world," he told me, "when something went wrong there was always a structure around it. Other people involved. Processes. It was easier to distribute the discomfort."*
>
> *"And on your own?"*
>
> *"On your own it is all yours," he said. "Which is actually clarifying, even if it is not pleasant. There is no one else to look at. You see very clearly what you did and what you should have done differently."*
>
> *"Did that help?"*
>
> *"It helped enormously," he said. "The pitch I lost made me a much better pitcher. The engagement that struggled made me much more careful about what I committed to. I would not have learned those things any other way."*

People watching a professional navigate difficulty remember two things: the difficulty, and the response to it. The latter, handled with honesty and composure, can reinforce a reputation in ways that straightforward success rarely does. Recovery, done well, says something about character that a string of easy victories cannot.

The Long Arithmetic of Credibility

There are no shortcuts to a strong reputation. Reputation is the long arithmetic of behaviour. Every interaction, every commitment kept or broken, every moment of generosity or its absence, every instance of intellectual honesty or its opposite—all of it adds or subtracts from an account that has no shortcuts and no resets. Over time, the balance either compounds or erodes.

What I can say with confidence is that the professionals I have most admired, across a long career, were not the ones who pursued reputation directly. They were the ones who pursued quality, integrity, and genuine contribution, and allowed reputation to emerge from those pursuits as a natural consequence.

Personal brand is not a buzzword. But it is not a strategy either. It is the sum total of who you are and how you behave, day after day, in the ordinary and extraordinary moments of a professional life. The enterprise called YOU INC. is ultimately measured not by what it says about itself, but by what it leaves behind in the minds of those who encountered it. Build that, consistently and with genuine intention, and the brand will take care of itself. It always does.

KEY TAKEAWAYS

- Reputation is not what you post. It is what people say about you when you are not in the room. Visibility without substance is noise. Substance without visibility is still enough.

- Success has an inbuilt learning disability. The approaches that produced yesterday's wins can quietly prevent you from seeing what today's situation actually requires.

- Talent opens a door. Preparation, consistency, and honest conduct are what determine what you find on the other side of it.
- Recovery reveals character in ways that success cannot. The professional who handles failure with honesty and composure earns a kind of trust that an unbroken run of victories never produces.

Reputation is built slowly and spent quickly. The discipline required to keep building it—to treat every engagement seriously, to prepare when you could coast, to acknowledge failure when you could deflect it—is the same discipline that the YOU INC. framework has been describing throughout this book. It is not a separate activity. It is the expression of everything else.

REFLECT ON THIS

1. If sixty people from across your career gathered in a room tonight to mark your leaving, who would be there—and what would they say? Is that the answer you want?
2. Where in your professional life are you currently spending reputation rather than replenishing it? What would it take to reverse that?
3. Think of a failure you handled badly. What would it have looked like to handle it with honesty and composure instead? What did the actual response cost you that the better one would not have?

PART 5
Staying Relevant

CHAPTER 11

When Experience Becomes Baggage

I want to tell you about a conversation that unsettled me more than I expected it to.

It happened at an industry event—the kind where people who have known each other for twenty years gather to catch up, swap observations about how much everything has changed, and eat food that is rather better than the panels deserve. I was talking to a former colleague, someone I had always respected enormously. He was in his late fifties, sharp, deeply experienced, with a career that most people in that room would have been glad to exchange their own for.

> *At some point the conversation turned to a young executive at his organisation who had recently proposed a significant overhaul of the way the company approached its digital presence. My colleague had opposed it.*
>
> *"The fundamentals don't change," he said, with the quiet authority of someone who had said this many times before. "Platforms come and go. The underlying consumer insight is what matters. I've seen these fads before."*

I nodded politely. But I found myself thinking about the young executive on the other side of that table, sitting across from thirty years of experience, trying to explain something that the thirty years were actively preventing from being heard.

The proposal, I later discovered, was eventually shelved. Six months after that, a competitor launched something remarkably similar to what had been proposed. It worked rather well.

The Trap Beneath the Credential

Experience is usually treated with reverence. Job descriptions ask for it. Organisations reward it. Individuals list it prominently on their CVs, and rightly so—it represents years of learning, of navigating difficulty, of accumulating judgement that no formal qualification can fully replicate. For a long time, I too assumed that experience was an unqualified asset. That more of it was always better than less.

But over the years I began to notice something interesting, and sometimes troubling. In certain situations, experience was not enabling progress. It was preventing it. The very depth of what someone knew was making it harder, not easier, for them to engage with what they did not yet know.

"Nostalgia is an emotional epidemic. It does not announce itself as nostalgia. It announces itself as standards, as rigour, as the hard-won wisdom to recognise a fad when you see one. And because it wears those respectable clothes, it is considerably harder to diagnose in oneself than in others."

Vikram's Reckoning

No character in this book illustrates this chapter more vividly than Vikram.

When I first met him, he was the kind of senior executive whose experience was his identity. He wore it the way certain people wear a well-cut suit—not ostentatiously, but as a quiet signal of who he was and what he was worth. He had earned it honestly. The career had been genuinely distinguished. The judgements had, for the most part, been sound.

> *Over the course of our conversations—the leadership workshop, the entrepreneur sessions, the gradual process of what I would call his professional reckoning—he had begun to see his own experience differently. Not as an asset to be deployed but as a lens to be questioned.*
>
> *"I had a meeting last month," he told me during one of our later conversations, "with a team of people from our digital function. Average age, I would say, twenty-nine. They were presenting something about the way our customers were using a new feature. And I realised, about 15 minutes in, that I did not understand the vocabulary they were using."*
>
> *"What did you do?" I asked.*
>
> *"I stopped them," he said. "And I said: I need you to explain that to me as though I have never heard of it. Which I had not."*
>
> *He paused. "Five years ago, I would not have done that. Five years ago, I would have listened, nodded, let them finish, and then told them what I thought based on a framework that had precisely nothing to do with what they were describing."*

> *"What changed?" I asked.*
>
> *"I ran out of the energy required to pretend," he said quietly.*

That, I think, was the most honest thing Vikram had said to me in all our conversations. And it pointed at something important. The performance of certainty—the maintenance of an expert identity even when the expertise is no longer current—requires an enormous amount of energy, which could be spent on something far more useful, like learning.

The Comfort of Familiar Patterns

Human beings are naturally inclined to trust what they have seen before. When something works repeatedly, it creates confidence. Confidence gradually becomes habit. Habit eventually becomes belief. And belief, if left unexamined, eventually hardens into doctrine.

This process is not without value. Expertise and efficiency are built on exactly these foundations. The experienced surgeon does not reconsider basic anatomy before each procedure. The seasoned negotiator does not start from first principles in every difficult room. Pattern recognition, built from years of experience, is genuinely useful. The problem arises when the patterns no longer match the territory—and the experienced professional continues to apply them anyway, because the alternative would require acknowledging that the map has changed.

When Questions Matter More Than Answers

One of the quieter transformations that experience ought to produce—but does not always—is a shift in how we approach problems. Young professionals, understandably, focus on finding answers because speed matters and decisiveness is valued. The ability to assess a situation quickly and propose a solution is how early careers are built.

Experienced leaders gradually learn—or should learn—that the quality of the answer depends almost entirely on the quality of the question. A brilliant solution to the wrong problem is worse than useless. It consumes resources, builds momentum in the wrong direction, and is considerably harder to unwind than a problem that was never addressed in the first place.

> *I said this to Arjun during one of our conversations, and he recognised it immediately. His consulting work had given him an unusually direct education in the cost of wrong questions.*
>
> *"I pitched to a company last year," he told me. "I spent three weeks preparing a solution to what I thought was their problem. Went in, presented beautifully, the room was nodding—and at the end their CEO said, very politely, that what I had described was not quite the problem they were trying to solve."*
>
> *"What had you missed?"*
>
> *"I had done a lot of analysis and not enough listening," he said. "I went in with the answer before I fully understood the question. Which meant I was solving for what I had assumed rather than what was actually there."*
>
> *He had not won that engagement. But he had learned something that no amount of preparation before the meeting could have taught him: the discipline of holding your own conclusions loosely enough to let the actual situation speak.*

The Generation in Front of You

Experience also encounters a specific challenge in modern organisations that deserves to be named directly. Younger professionals—the Aaravs and Zaras entering workplaces today—carry a set of instincts, capabilities, and expectations that are genuinely different from those of the generations that preceded them. They have grown up in a digital environment. They process information differently. Their relationship with institutions, with hierarchy, and with the nature of work itself has been shaped by conditions that most experienced leaders did not inhabit.

This creates a particular difficulty. The experienced leader looks at the younger generation and sees unfamiliarity. Sometimes they interpret that unfamiliarity as inexperience, or impatience, or a lack of the qualities that built careers in earlier decades. And sometimes they are partly right. But sometimes they are missing something important.

> *Zara said something to me once that I have thought about many times since. We were discussing a situation she had encountered at one of her internships, where a senior leader had dismissed a social media insight she had shared as "not how things work."*
>
> *"The frustrating thing," she said, "was not being dismissed. I can handle being wrong. The frustrating thing was that he had not looked at the data. He had dismissed it before engaging with it."*
>
> *"What did you do?" I asked.*

> *"I went back with more evidence," she said. "Twice. And then I realised that more evidence was not the problem. The problem was that engaging with the evidence would have required him to revise something he had believed for a long time. And that was the actual cost he was not willing to pay."*
>
> *She said it without bitterness, as a plain observation about how people work. And I found it both accurate and slightly uncomfortable because I recognised in her description the very trap this chapter is about.*

Experienced leaders who remain genuinely curious about what younger colleagues see—who approach generational difference as a source of information rather than a source of frustration—tend to stay relevant far longer than those who do not. This is not sentimentality about youth. It is a practical observation about where signals of change tend to appear first.

The Past as Reference, Not Blueprint

None of this is an argument against experience. The professional who has navigated genuine difficulty, built things from nothing, managed failure and success in roughly equal measure, and accumulated the kind of judgement that only direct experience produces—that person has something of real and lasting value. The argument is about how that value is used.

Experience used as a reference—a body of pattern recognition to interrogate, to question, to apply selectively where it is genuinely relevant—is one of the most powerful assets a professional can possess. Experience used as a blueprint—a fixed model of how things work that is applied regardless of whether current circumstances resemble past ones—becomes, gradually and then suddenly, a liability.

> *Meera had found her way to this through the unusual route of her four-year break. Returning to a professional world that had moved considerably in her absence, she had been forced to approach her own expertise with something like the fresh eyes of a beginner—not because the expertise was gone, but because the landscape around it had changed enough that she could not afford to assume it still applied in the same way.*
>
> *"The break was clarifying in a way I did not expect," she told me. "I came back without the assumption that I already understood everything. Which meant I asked more questions than I would have before. And the questions led to things I would not have found otherwise."*
>
> *She smiled. "My former colleagues who had been in the industry continuously—some of them were less current than I was. Because they had not had to question their assumptions. They had been too busy confirming them."*

The Value of Not Knowing

Aarav raised the question that sits at the heart of this chapter during a session I was running for his cohort, some months after I had first met him in that classroom.

> *"Sir, isn't the whole point of experience that it gives you answers? You are telling us that answers can be a problem. That is confusing."*
>
> *"Good," I said. "Confusion is where learning begins."*

"There are moments in professional life," I continued, "when knowing too much prevents you from noticing something new. When your existing framework is so complete, so well-furnished with experience, that a genuinely new idea has nowhere to land."

"So, what do you do about it?"

"You practise a kind of strategic ignorance," I said. "You deliberately approach things you think you already understand as though you do not. Not permanently—you are not throwing away your experience. But provisionally. Long enough to ask whether there is something here that your framework might be causing you to miss."

Naren had understood this deeply, and I think it was part of what had made his leadership so durable across such different conditions. When I asked him once whether there was anything in the modern world of business that he found genuinely puzzling—not frustrating, but puzzling, in the sense of not yet having a framework for—he thought for a long moment and then listed three things.

Three specific, thoughtful things that a man with 50 years of professional experience was willing to admit he did not fully understand. I found that more impressive than almost anything else he had told me.

Staying Relevant

The real challenge of professional life is not achieving success. It is remaining relevant after success. Relevance requires something that success does not automatically provide. It requires the continuous willingness to question what you know, to sit with uncertainty without rushing to resolve it with familiar answers, and to treat each new set of circumstances as genuinely new rather than as a variation on something you have already understood.

The finished product is the professional who has stopped questioning. Who has arrived at a settled view of how things work and defends it from revision. The beta professional—the one still updating, still testing, still genuinely open to being wrong—carries their experience differently. Not as a credential to be defended but as a foundation to build from. The experience is real. The wisdom is real. But they sit lightly enough to allow new information in.

After our industry event conversation, I found myself thinking about my former colleague for some time. He was not a bad leader. He was, in many important respects, a very good one. But somewhere along the way he had decided—perhaps not consciously—that he had learned what there was to learn, and that the rest was application. That decision, I think, had cost him more than he knew.

The 60 people at the farewell dinner in the previous chapter—the most durable measure of a professional life—were gathered for someone who had never made that decision. Whose curiosity, even in his final years of active work, had remained genuine. That is the kind of career worth building toward. Not because curiosity is virtuous in the abstract. But because in a world that keeps changing, it is the only thing that keeps you genuinely useful.

KEY TAKEAWAYS

- Experience becomes baggage when it stops being a question and starts being an answer. The professional who approaches familiar territory with genuine curiosity is working at a higher level than the one who arrives with the conclusion already formed.

- Nostalgia wears respectable clothes. It presents itself as standards, rigour, and hard-won wisdom. This is what makes it so difficult to diagnose in oneself—and so important to watch for.

- Younger colleagues are not a problem to be managed. They are a signal about where change is arriving. The experienced leader who treats them as a source of information stays relevant longer than the one who treats them as a source of frustration.

- Staying relevant after success requires the willingness to question what produced that success—and to hold the lessons of experience lightly enough to allow new information in.

The chapters of this book have described the YOU INC. mindset as a commitment to continuous investment, learning, and evolution. This chapter is its hardest test: applying that commitment not to a blank slate, but to an already full one. To choosing curiosity over the very real comfort of accumulated certainty.

REFLECT ON THIS

1. Think of a situation in the past year where your experience led you to a conclusion before you had fully understood the question. What did you miss—and who, if you had listened more carefully, might have told you?

2. Where in your professional thinking are you currently using experience as a blueprint rather than a reference? What would it look like to hold those conclusions more lightly?

3. What is one thing a younger colleague has shown you, suggested, or challenged you with that you initially resisted—and that, on reflection, was right?

CHAPTER 12

The Continuous Reinvention Mindset

The most dangerous moment in any career is not failure. It is comfort.

Failure, for all its unpleasantness, is honest. It arrives with information and demands a response. It insists, sometimes rudely, that something needs to change. There is no ambiguity about where you stand when something has clearly gone wrong.

Comfort is more treacherous precisely because it feels so reasonable. It whispers that the current version of yourself has been thoroughly tested and found to work. That, what brought you here will take you further. That, the adjustments can wait—not indefinitely, just a little longer. And then, one day, a little longer has become several years, and the world has moved in ways you did not notice because you were too comfortable to look.

The conclusion I keep arriving at is this: reinvention is not an event. It is a practice. The individuals who remain genuinely vital across the long arc of a professional life are not the ones who reinvent themselves dramatically at a moment of crisis. They are the ones who never quite stop reinventing themselves at all.

What Reinvention Actually Means

There is a version of reinvention that gets a great deal of attention. The bold pivot. The resignation post on LinkedIn. The leap from one world to another, narrated as an act of liberation and courage. I do not want to dismiss this. Sometimes the dramatic reinvention is exactly what is needed, and it takes real courage to execute it. Arjun had done it, and for all the difficulty of the 18 months that followed, I believe it was the right decision for him, arrived at in the right way.

But the reinvention I am more interested in—and the one I think is more widely applicable—is quieter than that. It does not require a resignation letter, or a career change, or a new venture, or a moment of public declaration. It requires only the continuous, deliberate refusal to become a finished product.

> **"Egoless passion and loving detachment means caring deeply about your work—genuinely, with full commitment—without needing the work to confirm who you are. It means holding the outcomes with something other than a desperate grip. These two qualities together are what make reinvention possible at any age, in any circumstance."**

Naren's Question

I want to begin this final chapter with Naren, because his arc across this book has been, in some ways, the most quietly significant of all.

When I first described him—sitting with the question of what remains when the role is gone—he was navigating a territory that most high-achieving people spend their careers avoiding. The board seats and advisory panels had materialised as planned. The grandchildren were a delight. The travel was happening. And yet something was missing, and he had been honest enough with himself to acknowledge it rather than pretend otherwise.

Over the months of our conversations, something had shifted in him. Not dramatically—Naren was not a person given to drama. But steadily. He had, at some point, stopped trying to recreate what had been and started asking what could still be built.

> *"I made a decision," he told me, during what turned out to be one of our last conversations for this book. "I decided to stop treating this phase as a diminished version of the previous one. As though retirement is the sequel where the budget has been cut."*
>
> *"And instead?" I asked.*
>
> *"Instead, I am treating it as a different genre entirely," he said. "Different rules. Different metrics for success. Different things worth pursuing."*
>
> *He had begun mentoring young entrepreneurs—not formally, not as a board obligation, but personally, in conversations not unlike the ones he and I had been having. "I have also started writing," he mentioned almost in passing. "Nothing intended for publication. Just the attempt to put thoughts on paper, in my words, about the things I had spent fifty years learning."*
>
> *"Is it any good?" I asked.*
>
> *He laughed. "Probably not. But that is not the point. The point is that I am still making something. And that honestly, I have discovered, is what keeps the light on."*

That phrase stayed with me. Making something keeps the light on. It does not matter what it is. A business, a team, a piece of writing, a conversation that plants something useful in someone else's mind. The act of creation—of bringing something into existence that was not there before—is what keeps a professional life alive long after the conventional markers of success have been achieved. Reinvention, at its deepest level, is simply the refusal to stop making things.

Identity Is More Flexible Than We Think

One of the largest barriers to continuous reinvention is not laziness or complacency, though those play their part. It is identity. Over the years, we accumulate a sense of who we are professionally. The sector we belong to, expertise we have built, and the role we are known for. These labels are not without value—they represent real things, earned honestly. But they can become cages if we are not careful.

The professional who defines themselves as a banker, or a strategist, or a marketing expert, has drawn a boundary around their identity. And boundaries, while useful for orientation, can make it harder to move when movement is required. The art of leaving, I have come to believe, is not only about leaving organisations or roles. It is about the smaller, quieter leaving that reinvention always requires—the willingness to leave behind a version of yourself that has served its purpose, to become a version more fitted to what comes next.

> *Zara had understood this instinctively, perhaps because she was young enough not to have accumulated the weight of a fixed professional identity yet. She described herself to me not by what she did, but by what she was trying to do—which was a subtle but important distinction.*
>
> *"I do not want to become known as a content creator," she told me once. "I want to be known as someone who understands how communication works, and who keeps finding new ways to apply that."*
>
> *"Why the distinction?" I asked.*

"Because content creator is a job description," she said. "And job descriptions go out of date. What I am describing is a capability. That travels."

She was 22 when she said that. And she had already arrived at something that most people spend decades figuring out: that capabilities are durable and titles are not.

Arjun had arrived at the same understanding, though by a considerably harder route. Stripped of his corporate title 18 months earlier, he had found himself having to answer the question of who he actually was without the institutional answer to fall back on. It had been, he admitted, profoundly uncomfortable.

"I had not realised how much of my identity was the logo on my business card," he told me. "When there was no logo, I had to figure out what was actually there underneath."

"And what was there?"

He thought for a moment. "Someone who is genuinely good at helping organisations think more clearly about complicated problems. That was there. The title was just the packaging."

He said it with a kind of hard-won equanimity that the Arjun of 18 months earlier would not have recognised. The reinvention was not complete—probably never would be, which was rather the point—but it had moved him somewhere more solid than where he had started.

Small Reinventions, Compounded

The reinvention that makes the most difference over the long arc of a career is rarely dramatic. It is incremental. A skill added each year. An assumption questioned each quarter. A conversation with someone who thinks differently each month. None of these feel significant in the moment. Over a decade, they produce a professional who is unrecognisable—in the best possible way—from who they were at the beginning.

The mathematics of compound learning work in the same way as the mathematics of compound interest. Small consistent investments, made over sufficient time, produce returns that dwarf those of occasional large gestures.

> *Meera had experienced this in a form that was unusually visible, because her four-year break had created a kind of before-and-after that most careers do not produce so clearly. The person who had returned to the workforce was not the same person who had left. Not because the break had transformed her in some mystical sense, but because she had used it—deliberately, purposefully—to build things that the relentless pace of her previous professional life had never left space for.*
>
> *"I read things I had been meaning to read for 15 years," she told me. "I had conversations I had been postponing. I mentored younger women in my network, which turned out to teach me as much as them. I sat with questions I had always been too busy to sit with."*
>
> *"And now?" I asked.*

> *"Now I have a better sense of what I actually think," she said. "As opposed to what I had absorbed from the environments I had been operating in. That is worth more than I can quantify."*
>
> *She had re-entered the workforce not as someone recovering lost ground but as someone who had quietly gained ground that her peers—busy, successful, unchallenged by external disruption—had not had occasion to gain. The reinvention had been continuous, even during the years that looked, from the outside, like a pause.*

The Courage Reinvention Requires

I do not want to make continuous reinvention sound easier than it is. It requires something real. Not the dramatic courage of the visible leap, but the quieter and perhaps more demanding courage of ongoing honesty with oneself. The honesty to acknowledge when a way of working has served its purpose. The honesty to sit with the discomfort of not yet knowing what comes next. The honesty to begin again—in small ways, repeatedly—even when the beginning feels unnecessary or premature.

> *Vikram had found this, and his journey across the course of this book illustrates it more fully than I could in a paragraph. From the executive who confused the reputation he had built with the currency he was currently earning, to the man who sat in a room of 29-year-olds and said "explain this to me as though I have never heard of it"—the distance was not enormous in external terms. He was still in the same organisation,*

> *still in a senior role, still recognisably himself. But something had been recalibrated.*
>
> *"I am enjoying the work more than I have in years," he told me, towards the end of our last conversation. "Which is strange, because it is also harder. I am less certain than I was. Less comfortable."*
>
> *"That does not sound strange to me at all," I said.*
>
> *He smiled. "No. I suppose it doesn't."*

The Conversation That Started This Book

I want to return, in this final chapter, to the classroom where so much of this book began. Aarav, in the third row, asking why his generation should plan a life around a single organisation. Zara, listening more carefully than she appeared to be, already carrying the weight of two futures simultaneously. The room full of young people who had grown up in a world so different from the one I had entered my career in that we were, in some important senses, speaking across a genuine divide.

What I have tried to do in this book is build a bridge across that divide. Not by pretending the differences do not exist. They do, and they matter. The world that Aarav and Zara are navigating is objectively more uncertain, more fluid, and more demanding of personal reinvention than the one my generation inherited. What I have suggested, throughout these chapters, is that this is not only a challenge. It is also, for the individual who is willing to take it seriously, an unusual opportunity.

In the absence of the old structures, something more interesting has become possible: genuine self-direction. The deliberate construction of a professional life—with all the discipline, strategy, and continuous learning that any well-run enterprise brings to its own development.

Where the Characters Ended Up

I think of Aarav, who has launched something imperfect and is learning from it. The platform is not what he originally imagined. It is better, because it has been shaped by what he discovered in the doing rather than what he assumed in the planning. He is still moving fast—that will probably always be true of him. But there is a quality of intention in the movement now that was not always there. He is beginning to understand the difference between restlessness and direction.

I think of Zara, who is building something that travels—a capability rather than a job description, a way of understanding communication that she will be able to apply across contexts that do not yet exist. She is still navigating the two futures she carries—her own and the one her family imagined for her—and that navigation has not become simple. But she is doing it with a clarity about her own values that I think will serve her well across whatever follows.

I think of Vikram, sitting in rooms where he is the oldest person present, choosing discomfort over the comfortable illusion of arrival. His reputation is being rebuilt—not from scratch, but in a more durable form than the one he had been spending rather than replenishing. He has stopped performing certainty. The relief of that, he has told me, is considerable.

I think of Meera, who came back to the workforce not as someone returning to where she had been but as someone arriving somewhere new. She has found, as she predicted she would, that being deliberate about what she spends her time on has changed the quality of the work itself. She is more useful to the organisations she works with than she was before the break—not despite the years away but partly because of them.

I think of Arjun, who has discovered that freedom is a discipline rather than a destination. The consulting firm has found its shape. The work is harder and more exposing than corporate life, and he would not go back. He has learned, the expensive way, that the YOU INC. framework is not about escaping institutions. It is about being genuinely ready—in whatever context you find yourself—to create value, adapt to change, and remain responsible for your own development.

And I think of Naren, writing at his desk. Making something. Keeping the light on.

A Final Reflection

Shoma read an early draft of parts of this book and said, as she tends to, something that was simultaneously encouraging and precise. "It is the book you have been writing for 40 years," she said. "You just did not know it." I think she was right.

The ideas in these pages have accumulated across a career spent observing organisations and the people within them, teaching in classrooms, having conversations on the margins of conferences, sitting with colleagues facing transitions they had not chosen, and occasionally sitting with my own.

In the process, I have framed many of my observations in my own lingo, so to speak—even if it may sound convoluted to some. They call them "Bhaskarisms"—in jest—and I have included many of them in the book as well.

The coherence is this: in a world that keeps changing, you build a far more durable form of security when you invest continuously in your own development—when you treat yourself as a dynamic enterprise rather than a static credential—than any organisation can provide. Not because the world becomes predictable. It does not. But because your capacity to navigate unpredictability—your resilience, your curiosity, your permanent beta state—travels with you, regardless of what the world does next.

The past has no future. But you do. Build it deliberately. Build it continuously. And never, for a moment, consider yourself finished.

KEY TAKEAWAYS

- Reinvention is not an event. It is a practice. The individuals who remain vital across the long arc of a professional life are the ones who never quite stop reinventing themselves.
- Egoless passion and loving detachment—caring fully about the work without needing it to confirm your identity—is what makes reinvention possible at any age. When identity is not staked on the current version of yourself, revising that version becomes curiosity rather than loss.
- Capabilities are durable. Titles are not. The professional who defines themselves by what they can genuinely do is considerably more portable than the one who defines themselves by what they are currently called.
- Making something keeps the light on. Reinvention, at its deepest level, is simply the refusal to stop creating—regardless of what stage of a career or life you happen to be in.

The YOU INC. idea is not a consolation for the loss of stability. It is a response to the reality of its loss. It takes the situation as it is and asks: given this, what is the most intelligent way to proceed? Twelve chapters have offered one answer to that question. What matters now is what you do with it.

REFLECT ON THIS

1. What version of yourself are you currently most attached to? How would your professional life change if you held that version more lightly—not abandoning it, but opening it to revision?

2. What is the smallest reinvention you could begin this week—a skill, a habit, a conversation, a question you have been avoiding? What is stopping you from starting it today?

3. When you imagine the final chapter of your professional life, what do you want to still be making? And what would it take to start moving toward that now?

YOU INC. – A FINAL RECKONING

The Complete YOU INC. Self-Assessment

You have now read the book. Before you turn to the Epilogue, pause here. Not to test your comprehension, but to test your honesty. The questions below ask you to hold the full arc of what you have read against the full arc of your own professional life. They are not comfortable questions. They are not meant to be. A well-run enterprise does not conduct its annual review in a spirit of self-congratulation. It conducts it in a spirit of genuine inquiry.

Take the time this deserves. Write what you think, not what sounds right.

THE WORLD

Looking at your industry and career right now: what is the Black Swan you are not preparing for, the Grey Rhino you are choosing not to see, and the Silver Lining you have not yet recognised?

What is the single most important thing the world has changed about how you need to work that you have not yet fully acted on?

YOUR ENTERPRISE

If YOU INC. were formally reviewed today—its product line, ecosystem, strategy, and infrastructure—what would the honest assessment be? Where is it genuinely strong, and where is it quietly struggling?

What is the most important capability you are not building? Not the most urgent, the most important.

YOUR IDENTITY

How much of your professional identity is tied to your current title, organisation, or role? What would remain—genuinely remain—if all three disappeared tomorrow?

What version of yourself are you most attached to? Is that attachment helping you evolve—or is it quietly preventing it?

YOUR REINVENTION

What is the reinvention—large or small—that you have been postponing? What is the real reason you have not begun it?

In five years, what do you want to be making? Write one honest sentence. Not a wish—a direction.

YOUR FIRST STEP

Having read this book: what is the one thing you will do differently, starting this week? Be specific. A general intention is not an answer.

Who will you share this commitment with? Accountability, as this book has argued, is not a weakness. It is the mechanism that makes intention real.

Before you read the Epilogue

The Epilogue is the final word—written in the voice of the man who built these ideas across a lifetime. It deserves to be read after this reckoning, not before it. So, close the notebook, set down the pen, and turn the page. What follows belongs to him.

Epilogue

A Final Word

There is something I must tell you before we part.

The book you have just read was not completed by the man who wrote it.

Dr. Bhaskar Das passed away last year, midway through bringing these ideas to their final form. He had spent decades accumulating the thinking in these pages—in classrooms and boardrooms, in conversations at the margins of conferences, in notes and messages and fragments of reflection gathered across a lifetime.

At the time of his passing, he was working on his third PhD doctorate, a fact that tells you everything you need to know about a man who considered the permanent beta state not merely a philosophy to teach but a discipline to live. He had finally begun the work of turning these ideas into a book. He did not quite reach the end.

His family, and those of us who had the privilege of working with him, decided to complete what he had started. Not to reinterpret it, or to improve upon it, but to honour it—to ensure that a voice worth hearing was not silenced simply because it was interrupted.

I have tried, throughout this process, to ask a single question at every turn: what would Bhaskar say here? In the passages that were his, I have touched as little as possible.

In the passages that needed completing, I have tried to write in the spirit of a man I came to know through his ideas—generous, honest, never quite finished, always still thinking.

But I want to end this book in his voice, not mine. Because the final word belongs to him.

What I have written in this book is as close as I can come to what Bhaskar Das would have said, had he been sitting across from you today.

For those who knew him, worked with him, or were mentored by him—and who miss his presence deeply—I hope this book makes you feel that BD, as he was popularly called, is right beside you, telling you all of this. And I hope I have managed to capture what he would have truly wanted to convey.

R. Sridhar

I do not know exactly who you are, or where you are in your professional life as you read this.

Perhaps you are young and full of energy and only now beginning to understand the terrain ahead of you. Perhaps you are mid-career, accomplished in ways you are proud of, and quietly wondering whether what brought you here will take you where you still want to go. Perhaps you are further along than that—sitting with the large questions that only arrive when the smaller ones have been answered.

Wherever you are, I want to say something simple.

The world you are navigating is genuinely difficult. Not in the way that previous generations were told their world was difficult—as encouragement, or as context, or as a reminder to be grateful for what they had. Genuinely difficult. The structures that absorbed uncertainty for much of the twentieth century have frayed. The certainties that your parents or grandparents planned their lives around are no longer available in the same form. This is real, and I do not want to pretend otherwise.

But I also do not want you to be afraid of it.

Because here is what I have discovered, across a long career spent watching people navigate exactly this kind of uncertainty: the individuals who come through it best are not the ones with the most talent, or the most credentials, or the most fortunate circumstances. They are the ones who decided—quietly, privately, without waiting for permission—to take genuine responsibility for their own development.

They are the ones who stopped outsourcing that responsibility to institutions and started building it from the inside.

That is what YOU INC. means. Not a rejection of organisations or institutions—they have real value, and working within them can be deeply rewarding. But a refusal to depend entirely on them for the stewardship of your own professional life. A commitment to treating yourself as a dynamic enterprise that deserves the same serious, continuous investment that any well-run organisation brings to its own development.

Invest in your capabilities. Not just the ones your current role requires, but the ones that will make you valuable across circumstances you cannot yet predict. Stay genuinely curious. Read widely, think across disciplines, seek out the perspectives that challenge rather than confirm. Build relationships through generosity rather than strategy. Manage your most precious resources—time, energy, attention—with the same deliberateness that a good corporation brings to its capital allocation. And review yourself honestly, regularly, without drama: what worked, what did not, what needs to be different from here.

Above all, remain in permanent beta. Never allow yourself to become a finished product. The finished product is the one that stops updating, stops questioning, stops growing. In a world that keeps changing, that is the one genuinely dangerous condition.

The past has no future. But you do.

I did not finish this book in the way I intended to. But I finished it in the way that life sometimes arranges these things—through the generosity of the people around me, and through the stubborn conviction that the ideas in these pages are worth hearing.

They are ideas I have lived with for a long time. I believe in them completely. And I leave them with you, with the hope that somewhere in these chapters you found something useful—

something that, at the right moment, will remind you of what you can build.

Your time starts now.

Bhaskar Das

About Dr. Bhaskar Das

Dr. Bhaskar Das was one of India's most influential media and advertising leaders, with a career spanning over four decades across strategy, media, education, and digital innovation. Widely regarded as a visionary, mentor, and industry transformer, he played a defining role in shaping the growth of modern Indian media.

He began his career in 1980 as a management trainee at Bennett, Coleman & Co. Ltd. (The Times of India Group), where he spent over three decades rising through the ranks to become President and Board Member. During his tenure, he was instrumental in driving the organisation's financial expansion, with advertising revenues and overall turnover witnessing exponential growth under his leadership.

Following his long stint at the Times Group, Dr. Das went on to hold several leadership positions across major media organisations. He served as Group CEO of Zee Media Corporation, Executive President at DB Corp (Dainik Bhaskar Group), and later as Group President and Chief Strategy Officer at Republic Media Network. Across these roles, he was known for his strategic foresight, execution excellence, and ability to anticipate industry shifts.

In the later years of his career, he continued to remain deeply engaged with emerging sectors, taking on roles such as Chairman of IdeateLabs, Director of Strategy and Insights at Craving Digital, CEO of Unica Token, and Chief Adviser of Exceller Books, reflecting his continuous engagement with digital transformation and new-age technologies.

Beyond corporate leadership, Dr. Das was a passionate educator and mentor. He taught at leading institutions such as SPJIMR and mentored students at MICA. He also delivered lectures at global institutions including Harvard, Wharton, MIT, and the

IIMs, dedicating hundreds of hours to shaping the next generation of leaders.

Known for his intellectual depth, boundless curiosity, and infectious energy, he was often described as a thought leader and an insight provocateur. His ability to combine academic thinking with real-world execution made him a rare bridge between theory and practice.

Dr. Bhaskar Das passed away on 15 January 2025 after a battle with cancer, leaving behind a legacy defined not just by institutional impact, but by the thousands of professionals he mentored and inspired.

About R. Sridhar

R. Sridhar wears two hats, both rooted in insight, energy, and expression.

As a Personal Energy Coach, he teaches his signature course, *Personal Energy Management*, to individuals, corporates, teachers, and students. Over the past twenty years, he has guided countless people to understand and elevate their personal energy, and is the author of two books on the subject.

In his second role, Sridhar is a book coach, editor, and writing mentor. A former Senior Editor at The Times of India, he reported to Dr. Bhaskar Das during his tenure, under whose mentorship he evolved as both a writer and a thinker, a relationship that continued well beyond his years in the organisation. In early 2024, when Dr. Das began work on his book, he approached Sridhar to write it, a responsibility Sridhar considers both a privilege and an honour.

Currently, Sridhar is empanelled as a Research Editor with Columbia Business School, where he helps academicians with background research work for their projects.

Through his firm, Energenie Academy, his mission is to create a million Energy Genies, people who live their lives by managing their energy with awareness and insight.

Website: https://rsridhar.com